Hans's Story

Hans's Story

Hans F. Loeser

iUniverse, Inc.
New York Lincoln Shanghai

Hans's Story

iUniverse books may be ordered through booksellers or by contacting:

iUniverse
2021 Pine Lake Road, Suite 100
Lincoln, NE 68512
www.iuniverse.com
1-800-Authors (1-800-288-4677)

Because of the dynamic nature of the Internet, any Web addresses or links contained in this book may have changed since publication and may no longer be valid.

The views expressed in this work are solely those of the author and do not necessarily reflect the views of the publisher, and the publisher hereby disclaims any responsibility for them.

ISBN: 978-0-595-45365-8 (pbk)
ISBN: 978-0-595-89677-6 (ebk)

Printed in the United States of America

FOR HELEN, HARRIS AND TOM,
THEIR CHILDREN
AND CHILDREN'S CHILDREN

Contents

INTRODUCTION

Herta., my wife, and my children had been urging me for years to write down what I remember of my life. I procrastinated, reluctant to undertake the big effort, but also not knowing how and where to begin. Then, one day some years ago when I found myself alone on a visit to San Francisco, I sat down in a deck chair in my daughter Helen's backyard and took out my small Sony dictating machine. I decided that maybe if I started by trying to recall the physical layout of the place where I had grown up in Kassel, Germany, other memories would follow. They did, with a vengeance.

Once I made myself remember all the details of our apartment in Kassel, other memories came flooding in on me. They came almost faster than I could dictate. They included events long forgotten, that I had no idea were still tucked away somewhere in my brain. That afternoon this History turned into an exciting journey of discovery for me, rather than the burdensome effort I had feared.

For some four hours in Helen's sunny backyard I just let it flow from the newly opened recesses of my memory on to my tongue and into the tape recorder, a stream-of-consciousness without much organizing effort.

Once I had this head start, I did not find it hard to finish the first draft of my German years over the next few months.

Then I had trouble getting back to it. Over the next few years there were so many other seemingly more important things to do. Eventually, however, the urge to get on with my Story returned. I dictated in Menemsha on Martha's Vineyard, in Waterford, Vermont and in Cambridge, and once again I found doing so a pleasure and not a chore. I talked into the dictating machine about everything: my student life in England and meeting Herta and working with her, life during the two and one-half years between arrival in America and enlistment in the U.S. Army and my almost five years of Army life.

By then, years had passed since I had dictated the first chapter, the one on my German years. When I re-read it, I thought of a good deal that I ought to add and clarify. I did so.

It all came straight out of my memory, with only two exceptions. I discovered a folder of my letters written between 1937 and 1939 from England to my parents in Germany, which my parents must have thought important enough to bring along to America. These quite amazingly mature letters from a teenager refreshed some of my recollections. Similarly, a history of the 82nd Airborne Division in World War II which I own helped me, principally with dates and names.

With these minor exceptions, the story that follows is pretty much as I dictated it from memory, more or less chronological but with flashbacks and other asides just as they came to mind while dictating. I have generally resisted my lawyer's inclination to edit and reorganize, hopefully gaining spontaneity.

Is it all accurate and historically reliable? I have done my best to make it so, but memory is fallible. It is subconsciously influenced by reading about events, by pictures we have seen and occasionally perhaps by embellishments and wishful thinking of long ago that now reappear as fact. I have tried hard to avoid these traps, but doubt that I have achieved perfection.

Yes, once I got started, dictating came easily, but in the end it all had to be transcribed, proofread, copied and bound. My friend and secretary, Joyce Holt, was of invaluable help in getting all this done. I cannot thank her enough for working on it so lovingly and cheerfully, though the effort was well beyond the call of duty.

I have got great pleasure from writing this story and thus reliving much of my life. It has generated within me a great new interest in the broader background of those unusual times through which I have lived. This writing is leading me to a lot more reading about those times.

So here is my Story. Enjoy!

1

GERMANY

1. EARLIEST MEMORIES OF HOME

My room had a balcony. I was very proud of that. I had the only bedroom that had a balcony in our family. I could look down on the traffic going by and, when nobody looked, could spit on people's heads or throw paper balls and bet against myself how far the wind would carry them. My balcony was on the fifth floor. It did not protrude from the house; it was set back in, so that it was protected on three sides. Above and behind the tall red shingled roof began. Nobody could look in on my balcony because the houses across the street were lower. I was at their roof level. In the summer it was more difficult for me to look out when I was small, because there were flower boxes along the front of my balcony, as there were outside virtually all of the windows. To me they were a nuisance but they added a lot of color to an otherwise drab business street. We were not the only ones who had flower boxes. Almost everybody else did too.

The department store which my father inherited from his father was on the first, second and third floors of our building. My grandfather had built the building. I think he built that large duplex apartment on the top of it with our family in mind. I don't think he ever lived there. I suppose succession within the family was taken for granted then. In fact, judging by what I see of German business these days, its backbone still consists of thousands of enterprises that have been in the same family for many generations.

Our apartment was on the fourth and fifth floors. It was large but because the building which housed the store was quite deep, the apartment took up only the front half of the house. Behind it were the administrative offices and bookkeeping departments of the business. And behind that was a roof garden where we could play and where my father did his early morning exercises. Our house was on the main street of the town with lots of traffic going by. There were streetcar tracks and the streetcars, which were the town's principal means of public trans-

1

portation, went by all day and all evening long, with a lot of clanking and bell ringing. I got used to it, like everyone else in the family, and ceased to notice it. I am still pretty oblivious to background noise, probably thanks to the traffic on the *Obere Koenigsstrasse* in Kassel.

There were three large bedrooms along the front of our apartment. Mine was the middle one. On one side was my parents' room and on the other side my sister's. Both those rooms were larger than mine, but my balcony more than made up for the smaller size. From memory, I would guess my room was about 12 ft. x 15 ft. and the other two rooms were perhaps 15 ft. x 15 ft. each. I wonder whether that is anywhere close to correct, or whether my memory has shrunk or aggrandized their size. There is no way of telling now, for American and British bombs totally wrecked the building during World War II. More about that later.

My sister Elisabeth, known as "Lisel", was born when I was one year and nine months old, to the day. My memories of her begin with her living in the larger room next to mine. She shared that room with our nanny. At first there was "Detta". I remember Detta only vaguely. I think she was with us for about two years.

Lisel, "Detta" and Hans 1923

After Detta came our wonderful Ida, about whom I will have a lot more to say. As children we thought that sharing a room with Ida was a privilege rather than a drawback. She went to bed so much later than we and got up so much earlier that she never interfered with our activities. And anyway, we were very close to her. She was the one in charge of us, but she was also our friend and our advocate within the family. There were connecting doors on both sides of my room, so that I didn't have to go out in the corridor to visit Lisel or my parents.

I might as well describe the rest of the apartment at this point. Next to my parents' room was a sizeable and quite elegant wash room for them with two basins and a long mirror, separated from their bedroom by a curtain. Beyond that was the bathroom, which had a tub and a hand shower. This was the only bathroom. There was no toilet in the bathroom, as was—and still is—the custom in most German houses. To go to the toilet one had to go out in the corridor and enter a separate room which was shared by all of us who lived on the fifth floor. That included Ida, the nanny, and the cook/maid who had her own room off the same corridor but facing the back. I remember the room with the toilet as having an open window winter and summer and being very cold in the winter. One did not tarry there.

When I say the maid's room and the toilet faced the back, I mean they faced a large rectangular open space in the center of the building. This space, at our fourth and fifth floor levels, was open to the sky. At the fourth floor level there was a large domed glass roof which, in the custom of the day, furnished daylight for the three business floors below. The front and rear of the second and third floors connected by galleries on both sides at that point, allowing the daylight from the glass roof to reach the ground floor. In those days the routine use of electric light during the day was not generally tolerated.

A broad open staircase with two turns in it led down from the sleeping floor to the living floor of the apartment. There, as upstairs, was a long corridor, L-shaped. Along the long part of the L, there were three living rooms facing the front. The one that corresponded to my parent's room upstairs was known as the "Biedermeier Zimmer". It was furnished with Biedermeier-style furniture and was used mainly for after dinner entertainment, card games and the like. It also was where the telephone was located. Yes, there was only one in that large duplex apartment. And that reminds me that in that Biedermeier Zimmer was also the old clock inherited from one of my parents' parents, which my father faithfully wound every night. It is the very same clock which I have been winding nightly as long as I can remember. I hope that after me one of our children will take on that rather pleasant task. Somehow the thought feels good to me that this old clock has been wound by at least three generations of our family, probably more, night after night; a tradition it would be good to continue.

Connected to the Biedermeier Zimmer by sliding doors which, when opened (as they usually were) disappeared in the wall, was the music room, which in one end contained a grand piano and chairs and music stands for chamber music. In the front half of that room, which corresponded to mine upstairs, was a tea table with large upholstered furniture assembled around it, which is where most comfortable sitting around took place. It was also the place where one sat to listen to music. There was a lot of listening to music. Finally there was the large rather formal dining room. It contained a large round table—mahogany I would say—in the center, which could be extended by inserting up to three extensions. Against the walls stood two large, multi-doored chests which matched the table and contained dishes and silver and glasses. On one of them rested rather permanently—and seldom if ever used—a silver tea and coffee set, which had to be polished frequently. The family took all its meals in this room, including breakfast.

Off the dining room, but connected by a "soundproofed" upholstered door was a large multi-purpose room facing the light court in the back. It was mainly our—the children's—living room, but, peculiarly, it was also the room where my father took his after lunch naps every day on a couch. During that time we had to be in one of the other rooms, usually the dining room. If we made so much noise that he couldn't sleep, he would take his very large bunch of keys, which was in a leather case which he took out of his pocket before lying down, and throw it at that door. "Sound proof" or not, we heard the noise and it made us shut up.

All these living rooms were interconnected. But separate from all of them, off the corridor and facing the back was the kitchen, the domain of our cook whom I remember as a red-haired woman called Elise. There may have been others, but she alone sticks in my memory. The short end of the L that formed the corridor was on the other side of the kitchen and led to the downstairs toilet and then to the two entrances to the apartment. One entrance was by way of an impressive wooden double door, which was reached by ascending to the fourth floor via a large staircase from the ground floor. It, too, got its light from a glass skylight, but one that was separate from and higher up than the skylight that lit the store. If you kept climbing those stairs beyond the impressive fourth floor apartment entrance you got to "der Boden", the attic.

I remember that attic as an enormous largely unfinished space used for drying laundry and storing materials. There was also "die Waschküche", the place where the weekly wash took place. Washing laundry was a big thing in those days, before automatic washing machines and dryers—although there were washing machines of sorts. A special washer woman would come once a week to assist the cook and the day maid. All the laundry would be taken up to that room in the attic where it would be washed by boiling it in a large tub with a fire under it. As I write this, I begin to doubt that a real fire was risked in that tinderbox of an attic. I do, however, remember the boiling water in which the laundry was stirred round and round by hand with large wooden paddles. Perhaps there was an electric unit which brought the water to boiling. Then there were rinses also done by hand. Each piece was then pre-dried by rolling and squeezing it by hand. This was a two-woman job, one twisting one way and the other the other way. Some pieces only, I believe—perhaps those which ultimately had to be ironed (which meant almost everything)—were then put through a mechanical wringer. After it went through the wringer, the laundry was hung up to dry on long lines going back and forth all over that large attic. This operation took the better part of a day each week,—"washing day".

We children were allowed to crank the wringer when we were around. We enjoyed that privilege, particularly because it was said to be dangerous. If you got your fingers between the rollers, we were told they would come out the other side flat as a paper dolls' hands. I even think that a favorite German children's book, Max & Moritz, illustrated graphically what childrens' hands that had been crunched flat would look like. That possibility added to the thrill, of course, and it probably has a lot to do with why I remember all those details of "washing day".

The ironing was done on the next day, I think also up there. The bed sheets were made of linen—they were certainly not fitted sheets—and they plus almost everything else had to be ironed. Perhaps there was some sort of stove with fire up there after all, for I do remember irons that were heated on a stove and had to be exchanged for the next iron whenever they cooled. The wooden handle snapped on and off as each cool iron was replaced with a hot one.

I said earlier, before I was distracted by my memories of that magic attic—such a wonderful place for us children to play and also to imagine weird things that might be happening there in our absence—that there were two ways to get into the apartment. One was by way of the grand door after climbing three long flights of stairs. The other way was the elevator which served both the store and our apartment. One had to have a special key to enter the apartment by way of the elevator door. Only my parents had this key. We children and the servants were expected to walk up. While the elevator served mostly the business, when we had guests another ground-floor door to the elevator at the opposite side from the business could be unlocked and guests could use that elevator to bypass the business and come straight up to our living quarters. Both grandmothers also had a key to the apartment entrance by way of the elevator.

While mine was the only balcony on the fifth floor, there was another balcony off the dining room and the music room. It was cantilevered out so that one could look up and down the street from this balcony. My most vivid memories of that balcony are of anxiety-filled evenings when our mother stationed us there to look out for my father's return on his motorcycle from business trips to outlying branch stores in the provinces. My mother always imagined the worst if he wasn't home on the dot of time. The roads in those days were mostly tar covered dirt roads, very dusty and slippery for motorcycles. I have no idea why my father used a motorcycle. I think he enjoyed the derring-do involved in motor cycling. He could have easily afforded a car. The business had several delivery vans. But I remember his green motorcycle, a "Wanderer" very well. Occasionally I was allowed to ride around the block with him on the back seat. He had a couple of accidents with it, none serious. He usually wore overalls on top of his business suit and, of course, goggles and a special but soft motorcycler's hat when he took off on that machine; no helmets in those days. It was fun for us to spot him by eye and ear when he finally showed up and to report his impending return to our mother whose face always lit up at the news.

That balcony was also the place from where, much later, the family watched with trepidation the more and more frequent marches up the main street of the militant arms of political parties, from the Social Democrats' "Reichsbanner" to the Nazi SA and SS. It was also the place where the flag was flown on special occasions. I suspect that, once upon a time, it was a harmless habit on festive days, like flying the Stars and Stripes is these days for many American families. But in the '30s I remember it as a touchy problem. Were we to fly the good old black, red and gold of the Weimar Republic or, as many of our neighbors did by then, the more nationalistic and right wing black, white and red of the Germany of the Kaiser? Of course there were also more and more houses by then which flew the swastika on a red and white background of the Nazis. That was out for us, but the black, white and red was a compromise with which some Jews could live. My recollection is, though this could be wrong, that we solved the dilemma by ceasing to fly any flag as 1933 approached. Anyway, that gets me a little ahead of my story. The flag problem is, however, a memory closely associated with that fourth floor balcony, for it used to be fun for me as a small boy to help with planting the staff of the flag in a receptacle that was built in at the rear of the balcony and then to rest it in a cradle which held it at the railing and from where it protruded at an angle into the air above the street.

Lisel and I played a lot with each other, and got along well most of the time. I can't remember many details about what we played and what toys we had. I don't recall her playing a lot with dolls, but that could be wrong. I had a teddy bear which accompanied me for many, many years and found its end only during a house cleaning in Cambridge, Massachusetts in 1991. He had lost one arm at some dangerous point in our far flung travels together. There were trucks and trains, I think, but it is difficult at this point to tell apart what I had as a child and what Harris played with. I do recall installing a Morse code message system between my room and my sister's. Believe it or not, even she learned the Morse code and we were able to communicate back and forth quite well, tapping out our messages much as they did along the Union Pacific lines in the 19th century. I still know most of my Morse code, to my great surprise. I just gave myself a test. I wonder whether Lisel does.

Hans and Lisel 1924

In the evenings, before my parents went to bed, they came into my room and gave me a goodnight kiss. I must have been half awake sometimes; how else would I remember this? I have a suspicion that I sometimes pretended to sleep when, in fact, I had been reading under my blanket with a flashlight. I know I did the latter. On Sunday mornings we were allowed to come to our parents bedroom and crawl into their bed. That included some roughhousing and bouncing up and down on them. I also remember, however, that there tended to be—and one took it for granted and took no offense—a slight smell of urine in their room, for my father used a chamber pot during the night which was emptied by the maid in the morning. Every bedside table in those days had the usual drawer for odds and ends at the top and a larger closed and often tiled compartment at the bottom for the chamber pot This habit must have stemmed from the days when there was either no interior toilet or an interior toilet so far removed from the bedroom that it was a chore to get there. This was not true in our house. The use of the chamber pot was simply customary.

Altogether, personal hygiene was different in those days. People, even well-to-do people with all the proper facilities, took a bath not more often than once a week. I think there was a theory that bathing too often was not good for you and your skin. As a result, there was much more body odor in the air. Classrooms smelled like locker rooms or army barracks. The same was true for crowded streetcars. I recall my father's bed sheets being quite sweaty and slightly yellowish at the end of each cycle before they were washed. I don't think bed sheets were changed nearly as often in those days as we take for granted now. And once again, this was so even in a house with servants to do all the work such as ours. Custom was set by those who didn't have all those facilities, I suppose. Which makes me think that I may have been wrong in saying earlier that we had wash day once a week. I suspect it was once a month, and that is why it was such a big affair. And, come to think of it, those huge German featherbeds probably also had something to do with all that perspiration in the course of the night. They still drive me crazy when I encounter them in Switzerland or Germany these days.

Everybody slept under featherbeds then. Our store had a big department, including a large machine which pulled the feathers out of used featherbeds, cleaned them and then blew back a mixture of the cleaned feathers and some new ones so as to achieve the preexisting volume. This was quite an important department. I assume from that, that people periodically had their featherbeds reworked.

2. OTHER MEMORIES OF PRE-HITLER KASSEL

First some facts.

My father, Max Löser (which became "Loeser" among English speakers) was born in Kassel on September 30, 1886. His parents were Ferdinand Löser and Marianne née Levy. The latter came from Hamburg. My mother, Cäcilie Löser (who in America became "Cecilia Loeser") was born on October 11, 1890 in Marburg, a small but well known university town between Kassel and Frankfurt, the daughter of Louis and Therese Erlanger née Gersfeld. Ferdinand Loeser was the founder of the department store in Kassel which my father inherited. My parents were married on October 4, 1919, shortly after my father had returned from service in the German army in World War I. I was born in Kassel on September 28, 1920 and my sister Elisabeth—known as Lisel—on June 28, 1922.

Kassel was then a town of around 200,000 inhabitants. There was the old city with a labyrinth of "Fachwerk" houses—houses showing their bearing timbers on the outside, with stucco in between—dating back many hundreds of years. Generally speaking, the poorer people lived in the old city. All our friends lived in the upper, newer sections of town, with one exception which I will mention later. Our street, the Koenigsstrasse, ran through the entire city, old and new. In the older part it was called "Untere Koenigsstrasse", and once it emerged beyond a large square called the Koenigsplatz, it became the "Obere Koenigsstrasse", i.e. the upper street. We were at Obere Koenigsstrasse number 27.

Our store, which extended over three floors, was not a full department store. We didn't carry hard goods like furniture and appliances, or ready-made suits or dresses. Speaking of ready-made clothing, in those days in Germany a large proportion of all clothing was either homemade or made by tailors or seamstresses to measure. It follows that our store had a very large "Handarbeits" department, which literally translated means a department for hand works. It actually referred not to crafts, as one might guess, but to all sorts of needle and thread work. There was a huge selection of patterns for making suits and dresses, there were endless bolts of material of all kinds and cutting machines which measured the length of what people wanted to buy and then cut it to the specified length. There was also everything that goes with embroidery and knitting; needles, thread, pre-stenciled patterns on material for cushions and the like. I also recall endless small drawers for buttons and other fasteners. Each drawer had a single sample of what it contained affixed to the outside. It was a merry sight. There was an employee who was the paid manager of that department, but my mother was really in charge of it. My mother was a working woman, the only one among our acquaintances that

I can recall. She was physically present in the department, on the floor of the store mostly, every afternoon. She did the buying and supervised, and sometimes helped with, the selling. She knew a great many of the regular customers personally and by name, and knew their tastes and likes and dislikes and their skills. Her presence and personality was an important marketing attraction, I am sure. In the evenings, over supper, my mother often reported to my father on who was in and whether or what they bought, and if not why not and what could be done about it.

I remember that department particularly clearly, because it was often necessary for us to run into the store to consult about this or that with our mother. I have greater trouble remembering other specific departments. I do remember that there were umbrellas for sale and a large glove department. I know there were blankets and lots of sheets and pillows and pillowcases, in other words everything for bedding, including the beautiful transparent containers that held many different kinds of the feathers which the machine, which I have previously described, would then blow into the bed covers.

There must have been lots more on those three floors, but it is difficult for me to remember specific departments. I remember ties and belts. Though I think there were no suits and dresses, there definitely were skirts and blouses, and sweaters for men and women and underwear for both. Then of course there was a large department of children's clothes. How could I have forgotten? All my clothes came from there. In fact, if I needed something, I just told my mother—or later on I just went down and picked it out and took it. I barely knew how one paid for such clothes. We were the local outlet for Bleyle sweaters and clothes. Bleyle has come to America in recent years. In those days it produced, as far as I recall, only machine knit woolen products. All my sweaters came from Bleyle, and they were truly indestructible. I had a blue sleeveless sweater which gave up its ghost only, yes I mean it, only in 1991. It must have been bought in our store just before I left for England in 1936. No such thing as built-in obsolescence at Bleyle then!

It is interesting to me how much I remember as I concentrate on those times and dictate this. At first I had trouble visualizing any part of the store other than the needlework department. Then, as I went on, more and more came into my consciousness, out of that storage reservoir deep in our brains, things that I hadn't dug up for over sixty years. Amazing!

My father's office was in the left rear, as one entered the store, on the ground floor. It was anything but grandiose. My guess is that it was 12 x 15, roughly, with a large desk and ashtrays and memorabilia on the desk, most of which dated back to my grandfather's times. A modern touch was that he had a window cut into the wall to the store so that, while sitting at his desk, he could see everything that went on out there.

I remember the black marble ashtray on his desk because I still have it. It has been in my office ever since I opened my first lawyer's office in Boston in 1950. Did my father smoke? Not regularly, I believe, but after a good meal virtually all men of his acquaintance lit a cigar. He did too. He also had some pipes around, but they, too, were used only occasionally.

My mother's brother Karl Erlanger returned to Kassel in the '20s from some years in Spain. He was employed by my father when he returned. He was in charge of the administrative operations of our business, including bookkeeping, and his office was in the rear of the same floor where our living quarters were located. He could come to visit through a communicating door to which he and my parents had a key. He was a nice but reserved man who never married. In 1933, as soon as it appeared that Hitler's rise to power was serious, he left for Argentina. He obviously must have chosen that country because of his familiarity with the language. He was quite hard of hearing as the result of an injury received as a soldier in the German Army in World War I. Sometime in the middle '30s he was run over by an automobile in Buenos Aires causing his death. This was a hard blow to my mother who, I believe, had been fonder of him than of her other brother, Ludwig. I have a feeling that Karl was a not very happy, lonely and, due to deafness, handicapped man.

As the previous paragraph shows, my thoughts concentrated on the store easily wander far afield to other memories which the store evokes. That's how I got to Karl Erlanger, and from there it isn't much of a jump to his brother Ludwig. He, too, had left Germany as a young man after World War I. He became a Zionist and was one of the earliest Jewish dentists in Jerusalem, settling there in the early '20s. I recall his telling us, much later, about his mostly Arab clientele and their strange habits and their custom of often paying him in kind rather than in money. He married a woman, Hannah, whose family had come to Palestine from South Africa. For reasons which are hard to fathom in retrospect, these early Zionists and well established Jews in Palestine decided around 1927 to return to Germany and set up residence and a dentist's practice in a small town near Kassel called Fritzlar. We went to visit them for dinner on Sundays occasionally, and they also came to spend holidays and other festivities with us. I remember them particularly strongly because they always, without fail, generated heated political arguments that tended to end in shouting matches which astonished us children greatly. I believe the subject of most of these debates was politics and Zionism and failure to understand my parents' and the rest of the family's commitment to Germany and to good German citizenship. But there were some other sources of friction as well, having to do with family finances. He must have felt that he missed out on this or that by going away. I do not know the details, but it was related to the distribution of some earlier estates. In general, Ludwig had acquired in Palestine—if he didn't have it before—an aggressive and rather uncompromising manner. He was good with us children, however. He was quite a warm fellow, contrary to his wife, with whom it was difficult for us children to establish a close personal relationship. They had two girls, Eva and Gabi.

This brother of my mother's, just like the other, Karl, left Germany promptly in 1933. Ludwig and his family returned to Palestine. He reestablished his dental practice there, but he and his wife separated soon after they returned. His daughter Eva died of cancer as a young woman in Israel, leaving three small boys (one of whom later died in an accident). Ludwig had qualities of a Jewish prophet, both in his unshakable faith in Judaism and in his uncompromising certainty that he knew what was right. In later years he wrote my parents, and still later me, endless letters in which he did his best to rekindle our commitment to Judaism and exhorted us, on pain of terrible eternal punishment, to become more observing Jews. I still have some of those long, almost unreadable but interesting and very well meant letters. He was a highly intelligent and well-read man and much of his learning was reflected in his letters. When son Harris and I were in Israel together in the middle '60s, we visited with him. I think that visit was one of the great pleasures in the life he led in those years, for he was lonely and not well understood by his daughters. I still remember our sitting in the sun in his little garden and talking about the family. He was most interested in Harris and his ideas and his future. I think Harris earned some of those long, illegible letters as a result.

To finish the story of Ludwig Erlanger, when immigration became essential in the late '30s, a family council decided it would be best for my mother's mother, Therese Erlanger, to join Ludwig in Palestine. At that time my parents were thinking of perhaps emigrating either to the United States or South America, depending more on which country would have them than where they wanted to go, and neither seemed a good destination for an old lady in her seventies. Ludwig at least had a house and was established someplace. So that is where she went and where she stayed until she died, I believe sometime in the early 1940s. I shall have more to say about Therese Erlanger in a minute.

To get back to the store, on which much of family life centered, it was, I believe, the largest store in Kassel except for the local branch of the Tietz department store chain which was two houses down on the same block. It was a real large department store carrying furniture and all that stuff. In those days such stores were considered "cheap" and were not frequented by my parents and their friends.

People like my parents bought generally in specialty stores. My father's suits, and my bar mitzvah suit, were made by a tailor to measure from material supplied from our store. One had to go to fittings before it was all done. My mother's clothes were made by a seamstress from patterns chosen from fashion magazines. I think the fashion magazines actually supplied some of these patterns. Banking was done at a Jewish private bank also down the street, whose owners were friends. In general, one purchased things from people one knew socially and who in turn purchased from us. Across the street from us was Reinecke's toy store and Metzger's leather goods store. One would not think of buying toys or leather goods any other place. Also across the street was a very good "Konditorei". There were at least three such coffee and pastry shops that I can remember within less than five minutes walk. Each was known for slightly different specialties and services and they were all frequented. Almost everybody went out several times a week for afternoon coffee or tea and a couple of pieces of cake. Most women met there in the afternoons, but my mother was not part of those circles. In fact, I don't think she went out for afternoon coffee generally. My father tended to dash across the street for a piece of cake, but I don't think he sat down long enough to have coffee. There was, of course, no such thing as pastries "to go", God forbid! Nobody would have dreamed of eating while walking in the street. Ice cream, of course, was an exception. It was sold and eaten in the streets. At a particular time of year, the pastry shops sold a precious specialty of the region, fresh "Speckkuchen", a kind of quiche with bacon. The real important ingredient were the particular herbs used in preparing it. That is what made it seasonal. These herbs were available only in Speckkuchen season.

I knew neither of my grandfathers. My mother's father, Louis Erlanger, died before I was born and my father's father, Ferdinand Loeser, the founder of the business, died soon after I was born, I believe in 1920 or '21. It is possible that it was the other way round. Both grandmothers were very much part of my young life, Therese Erlanger quite a bit more so than Marianne Loeser. The latter, "Grossmama" Loeser—her maiden name was Levi—lived stylishly in a rather elegant apartment five minutes from our house. She had a servant and led a very self-sufficient life. One didn't drop in on her uninvited. When we went we were dressed up for the occasion and were told to behave. She spent the summers year after year in the same two spas, Bad Wildungen and Bad Wiesbaden. In each place she stayed in one of those big hotels where all day long people wander up and down sipping the waters that supposedly have healing qualities. She must have had friends there who, like her, came year after year. The whole family did visit her in one or the other of those spas occasionally.

She also came to visit us for dinner on Sundays, always accompanied by her own cushion to sit on. Sometimes she came to listen to music at our house, and she went to the opera regularly. She must have been the source of my father's great musicality. I have the feeling that my parents', including my father's, her son's, relationship with her was correct and kind but not personally warm.

"Omi" Erlanger was quite a different story. She was very slim while Grossmama Loeser was very well upholstered. Omi had a beautiful face. She must have been a stunning woman when she was young. She was light on her feet and constantly on the go. She lived in a modest three room apartment on the Hohenzollernstrasse—number 37 flashes into my mind, right or wrong—about fifteen minutes from our house and came to visit often. Later on she developed *angina pectoris*. She sometimes had to stop on her way from her house to ours to sit down on the steps of some apartment house along the way to reach for the nitroglycerine in her handbag and put a pill under her tongue. It was quite a shock to me as a young boy when I first became an accidental witness to this procedure. That must be why I remember it. She told me not to say anything about it to my mother. I think I did not. She was a very warm woman, who did well with children. We loved her. We went to her house to search for Easter eggs at Easter and on many other occasions. She had no live-in servants, a relative rarity among our friends then, but a woman who came in to clean. I think her financial circumstances were quite modest. She and her husband had had a small dry goods store in Marburg. This is where my mother grew up. When my mother came to live in Cambridge, Massachusetts much, much later in her life, she occasionally drew comparisons between the two university cities at different times, particularly the differences between the revered "Herrn Professor" of Marburg and the "kids" whom she met with us who, nevertheless, said they were full professors at Harvard. I think my mother came to Kassel during World War I to work at a well-baby clinic which, in German, had the odd name of "public milk kitchen". I assume that its primary concern was to make sure that newborns received clean and nourishing milk, either from wet nurses or from milk that was processed at this place. I assume also that other health concerns played a role. This is where she trained as a baby nurse, a professional skill which she revived in the tough first years in America when she hired out as a baby nurse in households with a newborn child.

I do not know what happened to the Erlanger store in Marburg and how Omi came to live in Kassel. I do know that no family was left in Marburg. They were all concentrated in and around Kassel and that, by itself, may explain Omi's move.

While I am at it, let me mention some other members of the older generation that played an important role in our lives. First and foremost there is Thekla Erlanger, "Aunt Thekla". I wish I remembered more of her life story. It was an interesting one. I believe she was married briefly and then divorced, a virtually unheard-of tragedy in those days. She did not remarry and had no children. Yet, she became the family sage, greatly loved and respected. I remember her well, ensconced in a very beautiful contemporary glass and concrete retirement home. She had her own bright and sunny room with a bath and a small kitchen in the back. The whole front of the room consisted of a greenhouse. In other words, there was a glass wall looking out into a park and there was about three feet of space between the outer and the inner glass walls, with a sliding door inside. This was filled with flowers and plants. Meals were taken in a common dining room. It was a very beautiful and distinguished kind of old age home, called the Aschrottheim. We went to visit her virtually every Sunday morning. Though she had much authority as the wise old owl of the family, I remember her as very kind as well, with a twinkle in her eyes. I gathered from other people's conversation that she was accepted as the ultimate arbiter of family disputes. Her cousin, Dr. Felix Blumenfeld, a pediatrician, was the other great arbiter of family affairs. To my surprise, I cannot remember being bored as a child at these visits with a very old lady. She always had interesting things to say and for us to do. Sadly, in the final frantic rush to emigrate in the late 1930s, she was left behind. She may very well have decided herself that she was too old to face a new life in a foreign country. We believe she was brutally evicted from the Aschrottheim—which had once been established with funds donated by the Jewish Aschrott family—was deported and never heard from again—another horrible Holocaust story.

Hans on Day of his Barmitzwah
With Aunt Thekla 1933

Then, as I have mentioned, there was Felix Blumenfeld. He was our pediatri-cian. He was able to talk exclusively in rhymes with the children who were his patients. One of his poems entitled "Mein Junge" hung above my bed, framed, and above the beds of virtually all the boys I knew. I can still recite portions of that long poem which in a semi-serious and semi-humorous way encourage boys to be honest and not to tell lies. He could be screamingly funny and usually was when he came to examine you. Of course he made house calls. I can't remember ever having to go to his office, except for regular weekly visits in the winter to join a group of other kids who walked around circles drawn on the floor of one of his rooms, naked, while enormous ultra-violet lights surrounding the circle gave us a substitute for the summer sun. We had to wear dark glasses and walk the circle at an even pace, in the beginning for just a few minutes and later for much longer, maybe twenty minutes or thirty minutes. It was a strange ritual which, perhaps, sowed the first seeds of skin cancer in many of us. But who could have known?

"Onkel Fritz" Blumenfeld, as he was generally known, was a strong personal-ity who was heavily involved in Social Democratic politics. I believe he even served some terms as a City Councilor of Kassel. He was on a number of impor-tant Boards and almost anyone at that time would have listed him among the ten most prominent citizens of the town. Who could have predicted that, later, the Nazis made him clean the gutters of the street on his hands and knees, and that he was otherwise humiliated by the citizenry whenever and wherever he showed his face. He was too committed to Kassel and Germany to leave. The need for doing so was beyond his comprehension. This madness just had to be temporary! When he finally realized that he had been wrong and what horrible future lay ahead of him, he committed suicide. His wife, a non-Jew, stuck with him to the end, contrary to the behavior of many others in her position. I found her again when I came to Germany with the American Army in 1945. Where I found her was in the small country house in the hills above Kassel which Fritz Blumenfeld had built as an escape from hard work in the 1920s. It was called "Haus Heimgarten", which translates "House Garden Home". It was a beloved place which we all visited frequently. They were the only ones in our family and among our friends who had a country house.

Dr. "Fritz" Blumenfeld, Lisel, Aunt Thekla,
Leni Blumenfeld and Karl Erlanger at
"Haus Heimgartern" 1933

Other family members we saw a lot of included the Gruenbaum family. Mrs Gruenbaum was another "Thekla" and a good older friend of my mother's. She was a widow, I do not remember her husband at all. She was, I believe, Fritz Blumenfeld's sister. The family had a printing plant located near the rail freight yards, I suppose because that is where the big rolls of paper came in. I remember the great pleasure of being allowed to play in the cabs of their heavy trucks for hauling paper . They were green in color and had enormous rubber, non-pneumatic tires, and a shift and handbrake on the outside of the driver's cab. The drivers—and us kids who pretended to be driving—had to reach out of the window to shift gears. Thekla Gruenbaum had three children older than I: Ceci Hertzog, who is the woman I found post-Auschwitz in the Blumenfeld's cottage after the war; Rosemary, later Rosemary Heyman, who lived in Forest Hills, New York and has recently died in a retirement home in New Jersey; Kurt, whom we met much later again as a neighbor in Cambridge, and Franz. I vaguely remember as a child being at Kurt's wedding to Gertrude, who came from Worms. Their son Heintz—now our neighbor and friend, Henry—was the first newborn baby I remember seeing. Watching his diapers being changed is still vivid in my mind's eye. It must have made a great impression on me.

My sister and I both started school in a private school, the "Henckel'sche Privatvorschule" for the first four grades. Why a private school? I am not sure. My guess is that the public first four grades were dominated by kids who would never go on to high school and therefore set a fairly low common denominator for those schools. But on the other hand, the public high schools that we all went to from fifth grade on had mostly students who had transferred from the public elementary school system and did perfectly fine. So on second thought, I suspect it was more of a social thing. They didn't want us to associate with the rougher types, or perhaps it was that they didn't want us to have to put up with what these rougher types would do to us. I simply don't know. I do not think that anti-Semitism was a major concern in 1927, when I started school.

Hans going to school 1928

This little private school was, like all our schools—indeed, like virtually all of Kassel—within easy walking distance from our house. Our nanny took us at first, but we soon were allowed to go by ourselves. I don't remember too much about that school. I think I neither loved nor hated it. I went perfectly willingly and got average grades. As was true throughout my school attendance prior to Harvard Law School, I made no great efforts and reaped no great rewards. I got by with decent but not outstanding grades. Elementary school left no great impression on me. I remember mainly going to birthday party after birthday party of the children in my class. One of these constituted the exception to the rule which I mentioned before, that nobody we knew lived in the old city. One of the girls in my class was the daughter of the town's horse butcher, whose butcher shop was in the old city for the very obvious reason that only the poorer people bought horse meat. The butcher himself had become rich enough at it to be able to send his daughter to this private school.

The school was located on the "Weinberg", the "Vineyard Hill" of Kassel. There was a hospital next to it and after that came three huge villas all owned by the Henschel family, the biggest industrialists in town. The Henschel villas commanded a view over the big park, die Aue, which lay between the city and the River Fulda. The family owned the Henschel locomotive works which made many of the steam locomotives then pulling trains all over Europe. Later on they switched to building tanks for the German army and became one of the many German industries that during World War II used citizens of occupied countries and concentration camp inmates as slave laborers. They greatly profited from the shameful conditions under which these conscripted men and women had to work. At my time, however, they constituted the ultimate social pinnacle of Kassel society. When Mrs. Henschel drove up in her chauffeured car to shop in our store and to talk with my mother, the event was duly reported at dinner.

After graduation from fourth grade, I transferred to high school, the Wilhelmsgymnasium, only a stone's throw from the private school where I had been before. However, it was a very different institution. It went from fifth grade through thirteenth grade.

The German school system at that time had two very different tracks for schooling. There were the public Volksschulen, which went from first through, I believe, ninth grade. It taught no languages or advanced mathematics. The vast majority of German children finished school at that point, but most went on into a highly structured apprenticeship system which involved practical training in a factory, shop, office or craft, with additional schooling directly related to the chosen career. Kids whose parents thought that a more academic type of education was worthwhile and who could afford the minimal charges for an academic high school—DM 20 a month, as I recall—switched to one of several high schools at the end of fourth grade, as I did. Many of these left high school after tenth grade.

This was called the "one year maturity", a name derived from the fact that those who went to high school through tenth grade had to serve in the Kaiser's army for only one year, as opposed to the several years for the more common folk. Echoes of the U.S. practice during the Vietnam War? These students who went to high school through tenth grade were much more highly qualified academically than those who stayed at the Volksschule, but they were not qualified to go to university. Only a tiny percentage of all children went to university in those days. Those aimed that way continued at the gymnasium for another three years. Those last three years were very demanding ones. Highly qualified and specialized teachers treated more like "professors" taught at that level. American universities at that time granted at least one year's advance standing to German students who had completed the thirteenth grade, "Abitur".

My gymnasium was only for boys. All high schools were segregated by sex. Reflecting the Germans' liking for uniforms, all students wore a cap—they were required to wear that cap to school—which by its colors and stripes designated the school they went to and the grade they were in. The school year went from Easter to Easter. Each Easter one went out to buy a new cap and wore it proudly, a bit like when the gold bars of my American Army Lieutenant's uniform were exchanged for the silver of a First Lieutenant. Some but not all girls' school also required caps to be worn. The girls' caps had no visor. Your character, or I should say what we then thought we would like to project as our character or temperament, was reflected in the way that cap was worn. There were a myriad ways, from straight on the head like a US Marine's to rakishly over one ear or the other. Others who though of themselves as more sloppy and devil-may-care wore it on the back of their heads. I wore mine tilted way over my left ear most of the time.

The curriculum was structured differently than in our schools. For one thing there were virtually no electives. For another thing, once you started a subject you went on with it year after year. You never took something for just one year and then dropped it. History, for example, went on year after year following a structured plan designed to give a good overview of all history, from ancient to modern, by the time of graduation. Geography was an important required subject also taught year after year. The same is true for mathematics, writing, foreign languages etc. In my school we started Latin in fifth grade and added French in seventh grade. English was added in ninth grade. There were other high schools which concentrated on Latin and Greek and taught no modern language. Yet others concentrated on Modern Languages and omitted Latin and Greek. One made that choice, or rather one's parents made that choice for one, in selecting a high school. People headed for university, particularly for Law and Medicine, were required to have a lot of Latin. This is one reason why so few professional people of my generation in Germany could speak modern languages. We did get a lot of depth in the bread and butter subjects, more so, I think, than our kids do who tend to spend more time on more subjects but without the continuity that is possible when you must stick with the same subject over many consecutive years.

The teachers were highly qualified in their subjects. They all had specialized university training. On the other hand, I think they knew little about pedagogical precepts. Discipline was tight and was accepted as "the way things are" by everybody. For example, when the teacher entered the room, all children had to stand at attention until he gave the signal for sitting down. I can safely say "he" because all teachers were men in my school. You were expected to sit up straight with your hands on the desk. If you did something wrong, a slap with the teacher's ruler aimed at those hands was quite common. There was little personal rapport with teachers. It was a "we and they" relationship. All teachers had nicknames, many of them quite insulting and often mean, emphasizing a particular teacher's habits or peculiarities. Teachers were occasionally respected but never, never liked. Admitting to liking a teacher was against the students' code of conduct and, had it ever happened, would have lead to merciless ridicule. One played tricks and cheated as a matter of course. Being expert at doing so without getting caught conferred great status in the eyes of our student peers. On the other hand, the tight disciplinary system did not give much leeway and being caught would result in prompt punishment. The lightest punishment was, believe it or not, having to stand in the corner of the classroom with your face to the wall for a predetermined period of time. Beyond that you were given enormous, often ridiculous homework assignments, such as writing a particular sentence a hundred or more times. Or writing an essay each day for a predetermined number of days or weeks. Or having to stay after class. Teachers were allowed to slap kids in the face. The "Ohrfeige", i.e. a slap on the side of the face with the flat hand of the disciplinarian, was a very common punishment for children meted out by both teachers and parents. I do not recall beatings with canes at that time anymore.

Sports consisted mostly of required and highly disciplined gymnastics. I believe we had those sports classes once a day, or at least three or four times a week. (We had school on Saturday mornings.) We learned to use gymnastics equipment like that we see at international competitions today, including the horizontal bar, parallel bars, and the various types of upholstered "horses". I hated that stuff. I was not good at it and I don't know whether my inability to perform or my dislike of it came first. Many of the other boys seemed to have much stronger arms. They could pull themselves up on the horizontal bar and end up on top of it and then perform endless graceful but muscle intensive tricks. As I said before, this was not my thing. Being good at gymnastics was another important status symbol among the boys. There were also team sports, played mostly in the school yard after school was out. They included soccer, "Handball", a game like soccer but substituting hands for feet and requiring dribbling as in our basket ball, and "Schlagball", a game similar to baseball in its basic purpose but with different rules and equipment. I was better at these games than at gymnastics, but still in the bottom half of the class's ability. I think I was quite a pudgy boy in those years and not much good at sports. I was clearly not a student leader.

As before, I continued to be an average student in most of the academic subjects. Learning came easily to me, but I was not inspired by any of those teachers, nor did I develop the drive within myself to excel or even to make more than the minimum required effort. German was the exception. Writing came easily to me and I enjoyed writing essays. The marking scale was 1 for excellent, 2 for good, 3 for adequate, 4 was a failing mark, and 5 was hopeless. I got 2's in German, and 2's and 3's in most other subjects. I can't recall 1's or 4's.

My outside reading included a good many of the German classics, often prescribed or suggested by our school: Goethe, Schiller, Rilke, Shakespeare in excellent German translation. We also read junk: German detective stories and other thrillers. Oh yes, and then there was Karl May (pronounced to rhyme with "Hi"). He wrote over 60 books, all about the American West as he imagined it. Karl May never traveled to America. I must have had 30 or 40 of his books, each quite thick. His heros who appeared again and again were Winnetou, the great fearless Indian chief whose silver-studded rifle never missed, and white trackers like Old Surehand and Old Shatterhand, each with his peculiar and well understood strengths and weaknesses. And how could I ever forget Winnetou's great black horse which warned him of approaching danger, could run faster than any other horse and, in extremity, Winnetou could reach out for its "secret" by putting his hand between its ears and whisper "Rih-Rih". Then it would lower its ears and stretch into a super-gallop beyond anybody's reach. The Sierra Nevada was the imagined scene of many of his books, though others also took us to the Arabian deserts. All of us German boys loved those books and discussed them endlessly.

I did get a bicycle quite early and was allowed to ride it around Kassel. I liked that. I also liked working on the bicycle and attaching various gadgets to it—shades of the future. My bicycle came with tools to fix it. Beyond that, the availability of tools in our house was primitive. I still own the tool box from Kassel. I have no idea why it survived. I cannot remember ever seeing my father with a hammer in hand. Pictures were hung by servants; repairs were done by hired professionals who were readily available.

At some point, probably around age eleven or twelve, I was given a folding kayak for my birthday. This was a two-seater which was propelled by double ended oars. However, it was not nearly as tippy as the typical kayak these days. It had a broader beam. While it was "folding", the folding and unfolding was a lot of work, took at least an hour, and produced an enormously heavy package which was hard to manage. It was intended to make it possible to take the boat along by car or train. What made it so heavy was that the skin was made of canvas heavily rubberized on both sides in bright colors. The light and waterproof plastic materials that we take for granted did not exist then. I kept this boat at a boat house on the River Fulda, and could bicycle there, put the boat in the water and go paddling up and down the river with or without a companion.

I was on good terms with my Gymnasium class mates until well into Nazi times. We did things together after school and attended each others' parties. Being the son of the owner of the large Loeser store, that everybody knew and where everybody shopped, marked me as "rich" among my classmates, though some of the sons of bankers and professionals may well have been richer. We were simply more conspicuous. Thus, whenever the class needed a prop for a play or material for a flag, all eyes turned to me and I was expected by students and teachers to be the one to supply such things. It would be so in any small town, I suspect.

The River Fulda which went around the city surrounded by park land was one of two recreation sites for Kasselaner, as people who lived in Kassel were called. There were swimming clubs, to which many people belonged. They had different characters and, like our clubs today, catered to different types of people. In the Summer everybody went swimming in the Fulda and lounging by its waters. Much of the social life of teenagers in the Summer took place along the river and at those clubs. Ours was the Kasseler Schwimmverein. Its flag was blue and white, while that of the neighboring Hessischer Schwimmverein was red and white. My kayak flew the blue and white flag. Of course there was also a free public swimming facility supported by the city. The people in the clubs looked down their noses at the common folk who had to put up with much greater crowding along the water's edge than we did.

I remember Lisel and I having swimming lessons at our Club. She was much better at it than I. In those days the teacher had a long stick with a large loop at the end. After instructions on what to do, we were made to move out to deep water, hanging on to the loop the teacher dangled in front of us only if we couldn't stay afloat, but generally struggling as best we could with the loop held just barely out of reach. It was basically a swim or sink proposition, with safeguards against drowning but not against sputtering and taking in more water than we wanted. I was pretty scared and did a lot of struggling. Lisel took to it much more easily. Then, in the highly regulated fashion of German life, one had to take an exam which ended up with a certificate that certified that one had swum in deep water for a certain length of time. I have an idea, though this may be wrong, that there was a first stage which certified to fifteen minutes and a later stage that certified to forty-five minutes. Possession of these certificates was required for all sorts of things in later life.

The other major recreation site was in the hills above Kassel. We were lucky to have both a swimmable river and walkable and skiable hills in the immediate vicinity. There were very large parks covering both sites. The park in the hills, Wilhelmshoehe, is well known throughout Germany. At the very top of it was—it's still there—an enormous tower built of fieldstone with the oversized figure of Hercules on the top. One could climb up and even climb into Hercules's staff, which he leans on. It was visible from very far away and from most spots in the city. It was the symbol of Kassel. Beautiful and highly manicured park land surrounded it, with a complex system of water plays that started at Hercules's peak and then went via aqueducts, waterfalls, rivulets and fountains to a lake in front of the enormous castle which was the other major structure that overlooked the city from up there. It was fun for us kids to be at the top in the afternoon in Summer when the waterworks were turned on. If you knew the way and moved fast, you could almost keep up with the front of the falling water, all the way down.

While the side of the mountain between Kassel and the Hercules was beautifully kept park land, with green grass and well tended flower beds and decorative trees, on the other side, beyond the Hercules, there was forest that went on and on. It was great for excursions and long walks and runs. Since "going for an excursion" was the most popular family pastime in Germany, in which nearly everybody engaged every Sunday, this countryside was full of walking families. Most kids were bored stiff by these walks and moaned and groaned. However, it was taken for granted that they would come along and thus acquire the habit of walking for recreation, which was expected of each and every well adjusted family.

In the Winter, those hills were snow covered and we went skiing there. The streetcar which ran through the Koenigsstrasse right in front of our house, also went way up into these hills, passing through garden suburbs on the way. In fact, one line went all the way up to the Hercules. In the Winter, after school we could put our skis on the streetcar and go up there to ski. Of course, there were no lifts. If you wanted to come down you had to climb up first. This made skiing much more strenuous and much better exercise than it is today. On the other hand, it was difficult to become very proficient at downhill skiing, because one did so much less of it in a day. We kids usually went to a small hill, the "Schneekoepfchen", little snow head. We went up and down that hill and we also built jumping mounds where we learned to jump. Of course, we had wooden skis and it was the age before steel edges. Those skis would not have responded at all to the kind of turns we make today. It took much more effort and momentum. The turns were either the Christiania or the Telemark. The first involved a swing turn that was rather abrupt; it was not carved but relied on momentum created by a shoulder twist. It could only be done with more than a minimum amount of speed and in snow that wasn't too deep and heavy. With less steepness and heavier snow, the Telemark was the answer. There were no ski instructors or ski schools,of course. There were, however, parents, including my father, who had become quite proficient at skiing and took groups of us kids up into the hills and taught us.

My parents had an active social life turning, however, on a relatively small number of good friends, all families that had lived in Kassel for a long time and people that they had grown up with. Virtually all of them were Jewish. I remember the Schartenbergs, maybe because they were a particularly homely couple, he fat and bald and she with an unusually unattractive face dominated by a very large nose and sharp features. She was a particularly intelligent woman and one of my mother's closest friends. At the other end in the scale of beauty were their friends, the Liebergs, or at least Emmy Lieberg. She was the great beauty in their circle. Fritz and Emmy Lieberg lived in a small town, Ellrich, about 60 miles from Kassel, where their large textile factory was located. Visiting them was a Sunday outing. There were others, all either in business or lawyers or doctors, as I recall. No, not quite: Mr Sichel was an architect and his wife did social work. She was Emmy Lieberg's sister.

My recollection is that there was relatively little cross-religious social life at their level, but this has to be seen in the perspective of my reaching my thirteenth birthday in the year Hitler came to power. In short, I wasn't really of an age in which I would have been aware of the composition of their social circle in the mid—and late '20s, when the Nazis and their anti-Semitism was thought of as a mere nuisance and no real threat. I remember two events which make me think that their circle of acquaintances was much broader than I remember. The first is the celebration of the fiftieth anniversary of the founding of our store, which took place in, I believe, 1929. It was a big affair and high state and city officials, the entire power structure, took part. There were lots of speeches. There was also lots of food and drink. Representatives came from out of town, including manufacturers and wholesalers from whom we bought. There was even a delegation from faraway Hamburg. Historically, my grandfather's store had been affiliated with something called "Hamburger Engroslager". This must have been some sort of highly respected wholesale center that had serviced stores of this type in the late 19th century. The reference to "formerly Hamburger Engroslager" continued to be mentioned in advertising of our store, which makes me think it conferred some historical standing. I believe that was the reason for the Hamburg delegation.

I have much more specific memories of another great social event, a masked ball which my parents gave together with Dr. Felix Blumenfeld and his wife, whom I have previously mentioned. This was a big affair for which the largest ballroom in Kassel was rented, die Staatshalle. Invitations were designed by a famous Berlin artist. The words were printed in a very contemporary, multicolored style. A very clear picture of the four-sided invitation on parchment-like paper has floated into my consciousness as I write this. Have I seen it since? I don't know, but I feel sure that what I see was it. The people invited went far beyond the close circle of Kassel families that we later associated with. They included friends from Berlin and other cities, including some well-known artists, as well as a wide circle of acquaintances in Kassel. I suspect that this event occurred in the early '30s, perhaps 1931. It must have been an evening of great fun and as yet unencumbered by the shadows of rising Nazism. There were performers and very artistic costumes which people had professionally designed and made. I remember my mother in a black half-mask. I believe my parents went as Russian peasants, for I think that a Cossack blouse which I still own was worn by my father that evening. I can't swear to it. I do have an image of being allowed to come into their room to admire them when they were fully dressed. I was not at the party.

I remember often being in my parents room and admiring them when they went out in evening dress, with my father either in black tie (surprisingly called "Smoking" in German) or in his "Frack", i.e. white tie and tails. Kassel had an outstanding state-supported repertory theater, which performed operas, operettas and dramas. My parents had a subscription and went regularly. In those days in Germany one dressed for the theater. I believe that black tie was normal, but I also remember white tie affairs, perhaps openings. I suspect that I was proud of their elegance; why else would I remember those specifics of my father's dress?

We children were taken to the theater quite early, for the first time for special children's performances. My first serious opera was what I remember as a magnificent performance of Aida. Theater was an important part of social life in Kassel. When a great actor left or a new one was hired, this was talked about a great deal, much like the comings and goings of Red Sox players in Boston. The director of the theater was usually a famous theater person, and there was much talk about whether current performances under a particular director were better or worse than those under the previous one. There were also a good many lectures to which my parents went. You must remember that this is the age before radio and television. And there were discussion groups.

Talking of radio, I clearly remember when my father brought home our first radio. I can still visualize it: a small brown wooden box, maybe nine inches by nine inches, a crystal set with a plug in, glass-enclosed crystal on the top. One put on headphones and then juggled the crystal, which produced terrible static until all of a sudden, at one particular spot, the only radio signal in existence was found. It was a miracle! After a while, I was allowed to manipulate the crystal, for the station wandered and had to be re-found every time. I wonder when that was. Since I remember it, I suspect I was six or seven years old, which would make it 1926 or thereabouts. Later, of course, it was followed by vacuum tube-based radios with loudspeakers, which could get many stations and were updated by more modern models from time to time. All of them were installed in the Biedermeier room.

We also had a gramophone. I am not sure whether it came before or after the radio. It was in a tall rectangular chest that played 78 rpm records. It had to be wound, of course. We had quite a collection of classical music and opera. It never played in the background. When it played, one sat quietly in the music room and listened to the music. My father might follow it from a score on his lap.

Music was a very important thing in my father's life. He had a trained tenor voice and sang regularly in Kassel's *a capella* choir. We went to concerts of his choir from time to time. He also played the violin quite well and played regularly in trios and quartets. These music evenings rotated among the homes of the participants and quite often took place at our house. My father frequently practiced. The violin by itself sounded awful to me in practice. On the other hand, his singing which he himself accompanied on the piano sounded good. Whenever I hear Schubert lieder I have to think of him. I still recognize most of them from listening to endless practice. Unfortunately, I have not inherited his musicality. When my father went to a symphony concert or to an opera, he got a seat near enough to a light so that he could follow the music on the full conductor's score which he took along.

I had violin lessons from about age nine or ten on. Once a week I had to go to a doctor's wife, Frau Dr. Schumann, who taught me. I had to practice daily for half an hour. I did it dutifully and can't even say that I hated it particularly, but I made slow progress. My father worked with me quite a bit during those daily practices. He often got impatient with my inability to hear that the tone produced by where I had the finger on the string was impure. I took that violin with me to England when I was sent off by myself at age 16. I played a bit in England under the urging of Dr. Lewen, our music teacher there, but soon gave it up, never to touch it again. In retrospect, I wish I had kept it up. I probably was not as bad at it as my memory now indicates. I don't think my father would have kept me going if he had thought I was a hopeless case.

My father loved to travel. My mother tagged along on vacation trips, but, as she often told us, "preferred to sleep in her own bed." The family did a good deal of travel together, but sometimes my parents went on their own and frequently my father went on business trips on his own. They had no baby-sitting or house sitting problems. The house would keep running, and Ida took care of us. Our lives were little different when they were not there. Their principle constraint was leaving the store without either of them.

Once each year my father would go to a sanatorium near Dresden, the White Stag, where he, to his great pleasure, allowed himself to be subjected to endless indignities—as they appeared to me—like being immersed in mud, naked, and being hosed down, again naked, by very powerful streams of water. He took me along once, that's how I know. All this was supposed to be good for your health, a forerunner of our health clubs, I suppose. Me puffing away on my treadmill or Stairmaster going nowhere probably looks just as ridiculous to the eight year olds who sometimes visit. The White Stag was full of well-to-do businessmen who came there year after year.

Out of the deepest recesses of my mind, it just came to me that the reason I was at the White Stag resort and had the pleasure of observing all these naked men being worked on with water and mud was not, after all, that my father took me along. I now think it was my mother who took me there as a surprise to my father, perhaps a birthday surprise. My guess is that I was about twelve years old at the time.

My father and I 1936

My father was very health conscious. For many years, he exercised every day, in good weather outside on our roof garden and otherwise indoors. He used to wear peculiar short pants made of netting, which became dense enough to be opaque only around his private parts. In one room in our house there was a "Swedish ladder" attached to the wall. It was structured to permit all sorts of exercises, such as hanging from various rungs forward or backward and doing pull-ups, leg raises and stretches. We played on it; our father used it seriously and regularly. He was slim, with very erect bearing, to the end of his life. Our mother, too, was slim, tall and erect throughout her life, but she never engaged in sports or exercise.

My father also did a lot of horseback riding. He had served in a German cavalry regiment during World War I. I know he was stationed in Belgium during part of the war, but I do not think he saw any action. In the 1920's he owned a horse which was kept in a stable in Kassel's large park, die Aue. The horse had to be exercised regularly. I remember the business of having to get him out of his brown riding boots. He used a special gadget that hooked on the heel of one boot, had to be held down with the other foot, and then you pulled hard to extract the leg. Sometimes I was called to help pull. I remember the riding pants soaked with both his and the horse's perspiration, and I am afraid I also remember the horse hair encrusted in blood on the spurs. I think he used to ride in tournaments. I remember attending riding tournaments, but cannot recall seeing him in those tournaments and cheering him on. There were prizes, however, in the closet where his riding equipment was kept.

In that closet, too, sat a beautiful leather container in which his high silk hat was kept. It was like a jewel box with a fitted interior covered in red silk. The outer covering of the hat had short, black, silk hairs. Every time he wore that hat, my duty was to brush it with a special cloth to make all the hairs lie in the direction of the grain, which made the surface of the high hat shiny and mirror-like.

In the Summer our family usually went on family vacations to some faraway spot. We went to Switzerland repeatedly, usually to smaller resorts. I remember Churwalden, a small resort in the mountains above Chur. I also remember Hahnenklee. I suspect that the policy was to stay at the best hotel in a small resort. Perhaps, also, these small resorts were easier with children than the big ones, for I do know that in the winter, for skiing, my parents went to such fancier places as St. Moritz. We went by train to these places and often the last leg was by postal bus. What I clearly remember is traveling on buses that were open to the air, convertibles in effect, going up steep roads with hairpin turns and, at each turn, sounding their melodious, multi-toned horn. I suppose that is what would typically stick in the mind of a boy of that age. I also remember a swimming pool at one of these places, something that must have been new to me. And then, of course, there were daily hikes through the high Swiss meadows and into the mountains. These were hikes, they involved no rock climbing. There were cows all over the place. The huge bells they wore around their necks also impressed me enough to remember them to this day.

Our family dining out 1933

I remember many hotel meals served by waiters on those trips, though this was not a novelty to me, for on weekends or festive occasions we also went out to restaurants in Kassel. What sticks in my mind very strongly is that my parents, particularly my father, often ordered fancy dishes which were off limits to us children. My father loved lobster—which in those days in Germany was a very great luxury—and things like caviar, smoked eel and venison. It was taken for granted that we children had to make do with much simpler fare. My mother usually did too. I believe that was out of preference for simpler things. The same was true at home from time to time as well. My father, particularly for supper, often got things we weren't allowed to touch. One thing that I remember, God knows why, is a special kind of Gervais cheese which he would then mix with capers, chopped onions, paprika and maybe other things. Beef tartar was another dish that both my parents frequently had for supper, and it was similarly mixed at table with a wide selection of condiments. This, too, was not for us children. Perhaps we didn't even want it or like it. But there was one thing I did want very much that I didn't get. When we stopped for a sandwich at small country restaurants on excursions, my parents would order "Wurstbrot", an open salami sandwich on dark rye bread. The salami was piled on high, with one slice overlapping the other. For us only "Butterbrot" was ordered, and then four slices of salami which barely covered the face of the bread were added from the parents' sandwiches. I resented that and, as this proves, have still not forgotten these culinary slights.

We also went to the seaside some summers. There was a trip to the Baltic of which I remember very little, except that it took place. I do however remember well a trip to the island of Sylt in the North Sea. One got there by train via a causeway and we stayed in the largest town, Westerland, in the middle of the island. There was another town in the northern part of the island which was rough and much less citified than Westerland, called Kampen, which is where many rich people had houses built in the old fisherman's style, with thick thatched roofs. Westerland and Kampen on Sylt compared a little like Edgartown and Chilmark—or at least as Chilmark used to be—on Martha's Vineyard. The Henschel family from Kassel, which I mentioned previously, had a house in Kampen and we visited there. I mention this in part because I happen to remember it and in part to indicate that at this time, which must have been around 1931 or 1932, there were still no political or antisemitic barriers that kept the Loeser and Henschel families from visiting with each other on vacation. In retrospect, it seems like a last fling, for there was not to be much more of this.

At Westerland everybody, but everybody without exception, went to the beach every day. We stayed at a big hotel fronting the boardwalk. On the beach everybody rented high wicker baskets to sit in, which were used as shelters from the relentless and very strong winds. Every family also built "castles" of sand which were quite large, perhaps ten feet in diameter, with sand buttresses which also protected those inside the fortress from that ferocious North Sea wind. The sea, as far as I can remember, always carried a very, very high surf. We children were only allowed to play at the very edge of the sea. The grownups, of course, played in the surf and many fought their way through the surf and swam far, far out. In typical German fashion, that was considered the thing to do. I am sure there were considerable dangers and it seems foolish in retrospect. But altogether, in all kinds of waters, ocean, lake or river, I seem to remember that it was a point of pride on the part of every swimmer to swim very, very far out, if only to prove one's disregard for danger.

Such Summer visits of course generated summer friendships with families we met. For some reason I remember a family by the name of Devrien with whom my parents became quite friendly and, I think, my father had quite a flirtation with Mrs. Devrien. I can still picture her, a large, good looking blonde Valkyrie-like woman. Do I make these things up? Definitely not. Are they correct in every way? Who knows? It all comes flooding out of my memory as I write this and I believe it to be true. It is astonishing that a name like Devrien should suddenly appear out of nowhere.

The visit to Westerland had a very special postscript. During a walk to the beach, I am told I stuck my finger into water running down the street in the gutter by the sidewalk and licked it, my purpose being to determine whether the water was salt or sweet. It is believed that this act caused me to contract at the very end of our visit the then dreaded disease of "Scharlach", scarlet fever. It was a dangerous infectious disease, from which most children however recovered. Grownups, if they did get it, were thought to be in great danger of permanent damage. I was transported to the small island hospital and confined in a little separate building, the isolation ward for people with contagious diseases. Lo and behold, a few days later my mother joined me in that room, for she had been infected by me. We stayed there for many weeks after the season was over and the island had emptied of all but its year round population of fishermen. I remember my father coming to visit. He couldn't come in, for I remember him standing outside our ground floor window in howling gales, barely holding on to his hat and coat, and with a wool scarf around his neck. I also remember my mother complaining bitterly that the glass was so dirty that one couldn't see in or out. I had to take a rag to clean the glass sufficiently to be able to see our father and communicate with him by sign language. My mother and I had to stay on Sylt well into Fall. We both recovered fully.

These family trips to well established resorts stopped after 1933. It became difficult for Jews to take trips to Switzerland because they were generally not allowed to leave the country except for purposes of emigration and then only after paying the confiscatory taxes involved. German resorts very quickly closed to Jews. My parents did however find some remote places for vacations in the next couple of years. One time we took a "farm vacation", i.e. we stayed in rooms on a big farm and everybody helped with the harvest. The Sichel family, old friends of my parents from Kassel, were along with their two children, a girl, Annele, a year or two older than I, and a younger boy, Gerd. I fell head over heels in love with Annele that vacation. I followed her around all day long. Of course, I was much too young for her to show much interest in me. The Sichels ended up in South Africa. Mr. Sichel was an architect and very hard of hearing. Mrs. Sichel was an intellectual, active in civic and women's affairs. She became well known in South Africa as a liberal intellectual and a militant leader in the South African women's movement.

Another time after 1933 we rented a lonely house by a very large lake near Hanover, the Steinhuder Meer. It is located in flat, unattractive country but the vast expanse of the lake offered great opportunities for recreation. We rented a sailboat. This was my first exposure to sailing. I learned to handle the boat with my father. We both learned from the fisherman who rented us the boat, a day sailor with a mainsail and a jib. I seem to recall that the family was quite close on this vacation. There were no other people or distractions, and the sailing excited us and I loved it.

All of us on our sailboat, Steinhuder Meer 1935

Sailing for hours alone with my father was probably as close as he and I ever came before emigration. Neither one of us had ever sailed before, so we learned together. It put us on an even level—perhaps that is why I remember it as so pleasurable. It was not our usual relationship.

My sister and I were really raised principally by our nanny, Ida Beyer. We joined our parents for meals, having had our hands and faces washed and clean clothes put on before. I am sure our parents paid close attention to us and left detailed instructions for our activities, but they did not normally involve themselves directly in our daily play or other activities. They were there, of course, for birthdays and other parties, and probably at other times. But they were not the most important adults in our lives. That most important adult was clearly Ida. She was much loved. She came to us around 1924, I would guess. Ida was trained as a kindergarten nurse by the Froebel method, a well established German training institution for kindergarten teachers. She did not have a higher education, of course. She came from Westphalia, a town called Herne, but had grown up, and her family still lived, in a village just outside Kassel, Ihringshausen. As I mentioned before, she slept in Lisel's room and spent her entire days with us. There was no pre-designated free time on work days. She ate in the kitchen with the other staff. She played with us, helped with our school work, took us bicycle riding or swimming or walked us to parties at other houses and picked us up again when necessary. She read to us at bedtime and made sure we went to sleep at a decent hour and did not fool around too late after bedtime. She did have a day off, but I think it was less often than weekly. Even on her days off, she sometimes took us along to Ihringshausen, where we got to know and like her family.

For some reason I remember her thirtieth birthday. She got dressed up to celebrate it with her family and took us along. I distinctly remember her singing to us on the morning of that day the old German army song "Schier dreissig Jahre bist du alt …". The song is really about a thirty-year-old army coat, an ode by an old soldier to the coat that accompanied him through thick and thin. However, it was commonly sung on other occasions involving the thirty-year mark. I don't suppose I would have chosen to include this not very world shaking fragment of memory, if I weren't so amazed—and in a way pleased—that it survived somewhere in my head through all these years. No wonder I have trouble adding more to a memory so overloaded.

Ida Beyer got married around 1934, and became Ida Lichtenfeld. We were, of course, part of the wedding party, and not only my sister and I. Our parents were honored guests as well. I believe that she stayed with us for a while after getting married, visiting her husband on weekends. He was a large, tall and broad, very good-natured man who had an office job at a Henschel-owned coal mine. Eventually, he got an apartment in a company-owned house near Ihringshausen, and this is when Ida left us to live with her husband.

Ida's leaving was a great blow to both of us, Lisel and me. There were tears on all sides. In retrospect I know that this parting was particularly hard because by this time friendships and cordial neighborly relationships with non-Jews had become strained and mostly nonexistent. Ida was our most loyal friend and it was hard to see her go. In fact, my sister and I went to visit her regularly in her house near Ihringshausen. We loved to go there, and could do so by way of a lengthy streetcar and bus ride. Neither she nor her husband showed the slightest hesitation to have us Jewish children visit. That was very unusual from about 1935 on, even risky, and I am sure exposed them to unpleasantness from neighbors and perhaps other disadvantages. For them, decency and loyalty came first.

In 1945, on my initial opportunity after the end of the War to drive my Jeep to Kassel, I unerringly found Ida's rather remote location way out in the country and, yes indeed, I found Ida all well and in her house which had survived the war. It was an emotional reunion. She was more proud of me in my American 1st Lieutenant's uniform than any parent could have been. She knew a lot more than I did about what had happened to the Jewish families of Kassel. She had tried to stay in touch. The horrible end of Dr Fritz Blumenfeld, for example, which I reported on earlier was first relayed to me by her. Her husband, though forced to do war work, had also survived the War, but they had never had children.

Both Lisel and I reestablished our relationships with Ida and her family after the war and Lisel visited her in Germany whenever she was in Europe. She came to visit Herta and me in Cambridge at our invitation and even traveled with us to our house in Vermont. She loved it. When she saw our beautiful birches, she tried to make an extract from their sap and bark that was to stop my loss of hair. She was full of such homespun remedies. The last time I saw her she was in a nursing home near where she had lived. It was a well kept clean and friendly place, but she had Alzheimer's and I doubt that she recognized me. I went there with her older sister, Emmy, who had continued to live in Ihringshausen.

Emmy and her husband had a butcher shop in their house in Ihringshausen. When my sister and I as children visited the family, we enjoyed—or at least I enjoyed—watching how sausages and other meat products were made. We were never allowed to watch the killing of the animals. However, I have a clear memory of the enormous vat full of ground up meats of various kinds and juices, including blood, and Emmy Beyer's husband, the butcher, stirring it with his bare hands and arms fully emerged in those vats. I know that some people, after seeing that sort of thing, were forever cured of eating the product. I was not.

I want to get back to our daily lives in Kassel once more. Usually the family had all three meals together. We got washed and dressed in our respective rooms under Ida's supervision. I should mention that each of our bedrooms had a wash basin with hot and cold running water in the room. This is where most of our washing was done. As I mentioned before, one had to go down the corridor to the toilet, and baths occurred roughly once a week in the evening.

When we came downstairs in the mornings, the breakfast table was laid in the dining room. Of course, fried eggs and bacon or French toast were not part of a German breakfast. Instead there were fresh crisp rolls, which were delivered each morning in a cloth bag that hung on the door handle of the entrance door. There was butter and various kinds of jam to put on the rolls and a glass of milk. On weekends, there were soft-boiled eggs served in an egg cup and with a little knit cap on them, to keep them warm. To eat them, the knit cap was removed and the egg was decapitated with a knife. My memory is that it was always done just right, with the yolk being soft and flowing but not underdone. I doubt that my memory is correct on this point, but who knows. Then my father called the elevator and went down to his office. We children went to school, first walked by Ida, later walking or bicycling by ourselves. Everybody came home for lunch, which was really dinner, the main meal. I think, though I am not sure, that school went to one o'clock and on some weekdays resumed at three in the afternoon, usually with required sports and that sort of thing. This was also the time when those who were to be punished were held back after school.

Dinner in the middle of the day was a three course affair. There was always soup as a first course. Then followed meat and vegetable and potatoes, in some cases rice or noodles in lieu of potatoes. But potatoes were pretty much a daily fare and they were almost always peeled, boiled potatoes, "Salzkartoffeln", i.e. potatoes with some salt on them and "Petersillie"—parsley—sprinkled over them. That was pretty standard German fare. The food was served "family style", i.e. it came in dishes which were passed around the table and everybody helped themselves, although the grownups often filled the children's plates. The meat tended to be what we would today call overdone beef or veal or lamb. I think it was served sliced. I cannot remember my father slicing it at table, though I do remember him cutting up poultry at the table. There was also a big saucer full of heavy cream-based gravy, invariably. This was put not only over the meat but also over the potatoes. The vegetables were pretty much the same as we are used to. The third course, dessert, tended to consist of various kinds of pudding or fruit salad or both. All this was prepared in the kitchen and brought to a serving table next to my mother's seat. She then had to approve it and pass it around.

Although my mother did no cooking, she did approve the menus in collaboration with the cook and she did go shopping for food. Once or twice a week she went to the big open air market on the Koenigsplatz, five minutes down the street. Going to the market she was often accompanied by the maid to help select things and carry them home. There were nets which one took along in order to carry things home, for there were no paper bags, let alone plastic ones. These net bags had the advantage that you could ball them up and put them in your pocket when they were not needed. That way they were always on hand for spot purchases. Other shopping was done in one of several delicatessen stores nearby. We were well known in those stores, of course, and had charge accounts. We children knew that we could go into virtually any store in Kassel and simply pick things and say "charge it". This was taken for granted, but I must say I cannot remember ever taking unfair advantage of it. We did it when we were told to go and buy something, and not otherwise. One of the delicatessen stores just up the street from us had a big tank in the window full of fish. We loved to stand there and watch the fish. And we did sometimes have fish for dinner instead of meat. Carp was typical fish fare. It was boiled and brought to the table whole, including the head. My mother, not my father, normally cut it up. It tended to be full of fish bones, and I remember it as dry and not very tasty. I did not particularly like it. Sometimes we had what I think was shark, a fish with a lot of dark meat, which I liked much better. We children were disappointed when there was fish. Almost everything was boiled or roasted. Broiling and grilling was, I believe, unknown or at least not practiced in our household. Baking facilities obviously existed and were used. I can remember dishes of baked noodles with all kinds of ham and other meats cut into them, but I cannot remember any baked fish.

There was poultry, too, of course, chicken and on festive occasions goose. I remember boiled chicken in a cream sauce, usually served with rice. There was also baked chicken. A large goose was something special and it was festive, a special fuss surrounded a meal with goose. It was served with dark brown skin and had mostly dark meat, very, very rich though most of the fat had been drained for later use as a spread on bread. My father always made a ceremony of carving the goose. He used large poultry scissors. I can still do it his way, and found his method easily adaptable to turkey. Turkey was unknown then as a food. Goose was usually accompanied by red cabbage. I still like both very much. Fortunately at least the red cabbage is healthy.

We had wonderful cold fruit soups in summer. I loved those, and still do, though none that I have ordered since live up to the remembered taste of those days.

The evening meal was light, generally bread and butter and cold cuts. There would be a large selection of sausages and cheeses and, of course, very good German dark bread. My parents drank tea with this meal, which was served in glasses which sat in silver holders with handles. I do not remember what we children drank.

For dinner, the dining room table was covered with a starched white damask tablecloth. For breakfast and supper I remember a red checkered tablecloth of some sort. We each had napkins which were rolled up in a ring made of silver with our initials engraved on it. Fork and knife rested on a "Messerbaenkchen". This was a silver gadget which kept the eating end of fork and knife off the table-cloth. It made it possible to rest them there without messing up the table-cloth—really quite a useful tool.

I have been trying to remember typical table conversations. Mother and father talked a lot about events in the store that day. Later there was also much talk about politics. I think they asked us about school, but I believe our responses tended to be laconic—everything was usually fine. The theater and opera was an important subject of conversation between the parents. The reviews in the paper of the latest productions were dissected. There was also talk about the latest successes and failures of the businesses of friends and neighbors. Art, to the best of my knowledge, was not a major interest in our family.

After dinner we went to our rooms and did homework and then had to go to bed at the prescribed time. My parents either went out to visit or to the theater, or my father made music and my mother or both read books. There was no electronic entertainment, of course, but as described elsewhere, there was radio which progressed from a crystal set with only ear phones to quite competent tube sets with loud speakers, and there was the 78 rpm wind-up gramophone.

The kitchen which produced all this food was presided over by red-haired Elise. She was the other live-in servant, in addition to Ida. She was also the supervisor of the day maid that came in every day and of the cleaning woman who came periodically. All of this staff ate in the kitchen what Elise served them. We children, like our parents, took the kitchen operation for granted and did not take much interest in it, except when something unusual would happen. For example, an uncle, the husband of my father's sister Paula, had his own leased hunting preserve. In season, he would shoot hares and deer. Sometimes we would have one of these whole animals hang from a large hook in the kitchen. No, it wouldn't be the whole animal. There were no head or tails or legs and certainly no skin. It was the rump of the hare or deer that I remember. On such occasions we were not only allowed to come in and look and watch what was done to the animal, but I distinctly remember that I was permitted to assist with pulling strips of bacon attached to special needles designed for that purpose through the backs of these animals, presumably to keep them juicy when they were roasted. Elise was more of an authoritarian figure than Ida—though the latter controlled us much more and better than anyone else—and we were not personally close to Elise though she must have been with us for a long time. I do not know what became of her.

It occurs to me that, in describing our apartment in Kassel, I failed to mention the very important larder room off the kitchen. This is where all the food was stored. This is also where we had a big icebox, for which ice was delivered periodically. It was eventually, I would say around 1930, replaced by a Bosch refrigerator which was not so different from the ones we use these days, except that it did not have more than a minimal freezer compartment. But in the larder room were also endless rows of glass jars containing fruit and pickles and jams and other preserves that had been put aside when they were in season for use during the rest of the year. There were also racks of apples, as I recall. Then there was, but only in mid-Summer, "Dicke Milch", thick milk. This was milk that was poured into a bowl and left to turn sour. It had to be in mid-Summer, because only then, I suppose, did it turn quickly enough to assume a uniform Jell-O-like consistency. Sometimes it wouldn't work, would be watery and full of curds and had to be thrown away. But when it came out perfectly, we put sugar and cinnamon on top of it, and it was delicious. I think it tasted a little like certain yogurts, but not really. It lacked that yogurt-specific taste. Since nobody does it any more, I suspect that it can't be done, probably because it worked only with non-homogenized milk.

The other thing I loved that was kept in the larder room was "Schmaltz". There was goose schmaltz and pork schmaltz, the carefully collected drippings from the geese and pork we had eaten. They had the consistency of butter, but a rougher texture. The pork schmaltz had little pieces of roasted bacon still floating in it. I loved to spread it on black German bread, put lots of salt on it and then eat it as such or, possibly, with various kinds of sausage on top. Delicious, but as we now know, oh so bad for you. None of us knew better then, and we munched it happily. It's what we children made for ourselves when we got hungry in between meals.

Obviously, we children learned no housekeeping skills. We were not expected to make our beds, clean our rooms or learn to cook. Whether our mother knew how to cook before emigration I simply do not know, for I can conjure up no image of her by a kitchen stove. I suspect, though, that she did know quite a lot about food preparation, for she organized and supervised it. I have a hunch that she learned it in what was called a "Frauenschule"—a finishing school that young women went to after school and well before marriage.

My interest in cars goes back to those days. We had no private car when I was a small boy. As I mentioned before, my father had a green Wanderer motorcycle, which was parked in a back alley behind the store. I sat on it endlessly pretending that I was going places. I knew where all the controls were. In fact, I remember sitting in a chair in our music room with the piano stool between my legs. The seat of the piano stool turned to adjust its height. I used it as a steering wheel and took long trips on endless roads sitting in that chair turning that "steering wheel" and leaning into curves. And then there were the several delivery vans of various sizes which the store owned. They were parked at a nearby lot on Sundays and holidays, and I could go there and clamber all over them, sit in the driver's seats and go on wonderful make believe journeys.

There was still a lot of live horse power in daily use in those days in Germany. I remember the very beer wagons pulled by huge horses that we now see on Budweiser ads. But much other local transportation of goods still took place by horse drawn cart. I do not remember that taxis or other people movers were horse drawn. Much later, when the German army was being rebuilt and did much marching through the streets, it, too, still had a lot of horses. The officers rode on horses. Much of the artillery was pulled by horses. But I suppose in those times, the late '20s, George Patton as a U.S. Army officer also paraded around on horseback. Anyway, when I was in my room on my balcony, the clip clop of horse hooves on our street was quite a usual noise which did not attract particular attention. And horse droppings were all over the streets.

As I said, we didn't have a private car when I was little, nor did most of our friends. The only ones who early on had private cars was the Oppenheim family, my father's sister, Paula, and her husband, Viktor Oppenheim. They were considered much richer than we. They had a factory where horsehair was processed and spun. I know it produced the stuffing for pillowcases, for I slept on a horsehair pillow every night. All of us did. They were flat and hard and considered "healthy". Mattresses, too, were stuffed with horsehair, as was upholstered furniture. I am sure the Oppenheim's horse hair was used for other things as well, but I don't know what. It must have been in demand, because Victor Oppenheim started a successful horsehair factory in Switzerland as an anchor to windward soon after Hitler came to power, and after emigration to Switzerland started another in Northern England for his son Kurt to run.

The Oppenheims lived in a very elegant villa about ten minutes walk from our house, with a large garden. They had three children, the youngest of whom, Kurt, was about my age. Then there was Walter, a couple of years older and Trudy, the older sister. My father's sister Paula was one of the first women in Kassel to drive a car. This was still considered quite unusual. Like my father, she rode horseback a lot. I think I can remember her riding side-saddle, as behooved a lady, in a black flowing skirt. Both she and her husband had Mercedes Benz cars, one a convertible. This impressed me greatly. Actually, private passenger cars were of limited usefulness in those days. They were principally used to drive around the city and for day trips into the outskirts. It was not practical to take long trips by car, unless you were very sporting and trying to prove a point. The railroad service was superb, but there were no long distance, high speed roads. Most of the roads were dirt and gravel surfaced. The best ones had a tar finish on top of the dirt and gravel. To take a trip from Kassel to Frankfurt, a distance of perhaps 150 miles, which we now do on the autobahn in about two hours, in those days would have probably taken an entire day. It could have taken longer, for there would almost certainly have been prolonged delays caused by flat tires that had to be fixed. One expected to suffer frequent flats, as I recall. This must have had to do partly with the conditions of the roads and partly with the kinds of tires used. Thus, train travel was the only reliable form of long distance travel.

I saw quite a bit of my cousin Kurt when we were both boys in Kassel. He emigrated to London. Walter and Trudi emigrated to Israel.

I can remember many times seeing my father or both my parents off at Kassel's railway station when they went on business or vacation trips. Kassel's was a "Sackbahhof", literally translated a sack station. Less literally translated it was a dead end station where trains that came in had to go out the way they came in. The locomotive that pulled them in remained behind and a new one had to be hitched to pull the train out again. That, too, was fun to watch. As I have said, train travel was taken for granted for extended journeys.

Nevertheless, in the late '20s, my guess would be 1927 or 1928, my father decided that we, too, should have a private car. He took me along on all the inspections of possible cars and the test drives. The two test drives I remember—God knows why—were of a Buick and a DeSoto. Why would we seriously consider an American car? I have no idea. I do think my father did consider it seriously, though in the end I remember my father saying that he didn't like the "bauchige" shape of those Americans. The word means belly-like, and what he meant was that the sides of these cars were curved along the horizontal axis, they bulged out and had curves, while many German cars were still built with straight sheet metal sides and sharp edges. The only reason I mention this comment of my father is that I am astonished and impressed that this particular and quite unusual—if not home-made—German expression, "bauchig", should float into my consciousness at this moment, together with his personal evaluation of American car styling of that day. I doubt that this is something I have thought about between then and now, a time gap of close to sixty-five years.

We ended up buying a rare car that I had never heard of and that few people would remember today. It was called a Simson Supra. It was made by a factory in a town not too far from Kassel called Suhl. My father I think knew the owners of that factory, a Jewish family called Simson. They also manufactured hunting rifles and other arms. I remember going there with him twice. The first time we went to decide on all the specifications of the car which was to be built to order for us. We picked grey checkered upholstery from bolts of cloth. We picked a black color for the main body with a grey stripe around the car's midriff, from color samples. We had a choice of horn ring on the steering wheel or a horn button in the middle of the steering wheel. We chose the horn ring. We specified things like types of lights and the types of direction indicators. Most cars in those days had no direction indicators. They were still a very new-fangled thing. Flashing directional lights were, I believe, rare in Germany until after the War. The most modern device then was a red arm, about nine inches in length in a black housing with a light bulb inside. When activated, the arm swung out to a horizontal position and lit up. It could be installed in the post between the doors on each side or on the windshield supports in front. We chose the latter. We could even specify where the control would be installed. It ended up on the dashboard near the center, but a little further towards the driver's side. No, it didn't cancel automatically. There were undoubtedly other more technical things that had to be specified, but I either don't remember or, more likely, was not consulted concerning them.

My father had been taking driving lessons for weeks and finally the day came on which we, I think it was only he and I, took the train to Suhl to pick up the vehicle. It was very exciting to find it sitting there, all shiny and polished and waiting for us. One of the owners of the factory, a very fat gentleman, was there to welcome us, to guide us to the car and he himself explained all the controls to us. Then he took us for a spin around Suhl, with him driving and my father sitting next to him, observing and being instructed. I took it all in from the back seat. Finally,—I assume after a check had passed hands, we drove off. The trip must have gone smoothly. I do not remember any particulars of that trip or of our arrival in front of our house where this majestic, large car must have created quite a sensation. Those things were noticed in Kassel!.

My father and sister with our first car, a rare "Simpson Supra" 1928

I do have many, many memories of trips we took in the following years in that car, usually on weekends to go into the nearby woods for our family walks. We also went to visit friends in nearby towns. The roads were incredibly dusty. Each car trailed a cloud of dust. Tailgating was unthinkable. As I said before, there were many flats. The car carried two spare wheels on the outside, one on each side mounted on the fenders. Changing wheels was not much different from what it is today, though the jacks were more primitive and one lived in constant fear that the car would roll off the jack at the most critical moment. For us children, the main job was collecting the rocks that had to be placed in front of and behind each wheel to prevent such a catastrophe.

Another thing that was very different in those days was finding one's way. It was a big problem, that caused much discussion—sometimes heated—in the car, and many "I-told-you-so's". There were very few directional signs. At each intersection, I remember our stopping and trying to figure out where on the map we might be. When you found yourself behind a slow car, there was much debate with my mother as to whether we should approach braving the cloud of dust so as to pass it, or remain well behind. We usually ended up passing, for our car was a much more powerful vehicle than most of the others on the road in those days.

Passing, however, was an adventure on those sparsely traveled but dusty and winding roads. My sister, unfortunately, suffered from car sickness. Every now and then we had to stop the car to allow her to recover or, if things were real bad, to throw up. We must have felt sorry for her but, in so far as I can remember, never sorry enough to cut back on these weekend outings. She suffered quite a bit, I think.

Train travel has changed much less between those days and now. Of course, there are now very fast trains, but the quality of the journey was pretty much the same as going on European trains these days. They were the same first and third class compartments off long corridors. I do remember the dining cars of those days. They were very elegant. One was served on china that was especially heavy and designed in shapes that would reduce spilling. I remember big meals eaten in German dining cars, at tables with white cloths and well trained waiters. There was always soup, a fish course, a meat course and dessert. Bottles for wine and water were held in place by rings that folded down from the walls. It was great fun to sit and eat and watch the country rush by.

My parents had, I am sure, a good marriage. There were strains, for I remember sometimes being the unwitting witness to shouting in their bedroom next door. But their marriage stood the test of good times and of very bad times successfully. Of course I was closest as an adult observer in America in the first couple of years, where we all lived together in very close quarters in Long Island City and Jackson Heights. In the German years I was probably too young to be a conscious observer, but had there been important strains, I, as most children, would, I think, have noticed or felt it. I have no such memories.

They were very different personalities. My father was outgoing and loved parties and entertainment. He greatly enjoyed travel. My mother tended to keep people at a distance. She took real interest in people, was polite and correct with them and was an excellent observer of others. Yes, she was primarily an observer, not a person who would throw herself with abandon into human relationships. There was an untouchable core of privacy, I am almost tempted to say majesty, which people sensed and which kept them from coming too close. I think she knew that part of her make-up full well and liked it that way. The department head-to-customer relationships which she developed in large numbers in her department of our store suited her to a T. So did her relationships with sick and poor people whom she helped in very personal ways, of whom there were many. Beyond her immediate family, I think she was most comfortable with such productive but arms-length human contacts,

Leaving the day-to-day care taking of us children to servants was, of course, the usual thing in those days for people of my parents wealth. Our mother supervised us and our doings with loving care, but the key word is "supervised". The hands-on contacts were limited. As children we gladly and fully confided in Ida but far more rarely in our mother. Our father perhaps a bit more readily. She was also more of the disciplinarian than our father. In retrospect, I am pretty sure that she more than our father called the shots within the family. She ran things well and smoothly. Her enormous internal strength was crucial in holding the family together in the very, very difficult years to come.

Lisel, our mother and I, 1935

I know she accompanied my father on at least one skiing trip to Switzerland. I believe they both skied there. Walter and Ceci Hertzog—about whom more later—were on that same trip, but as I write this I realize that I remember this because of a photo in some album that shows the four of them on a train station in Switzerland. This reminds me how careful one has to be in accepting memories such as these. Undoubtedly, most are real first hand memories, direct from brain to page; others have taken side trips via photographs or later conversations back into the brain and thence to this page. They are impossible to tell apart. As I have mentioned much earlier, I do remember skiing with my father in the hills outside Kassel. I do not remember skiing with my mother.

My father had a frivolous side, which my mother totally lacked. Sometimes he got us children involved, such as when he shared with me the pleasures of selecting a car or would say, when I wandered into the store some afternoon, "let's go have an ice cream together". Ice cream, as I remember it from those days, came sandwiched between two waffle-like cookies. One could buy it from a cart in the street. This was mostly for children, and most respectable grownups would not be seen in the street licking ice cream. My father defied that tradition. My mother never would have. He got an enormous amount of pleasure from music. As I have mentioned, he was an active participant as a singer and a violin player. But he also was a listener. He could wax with great enthusiasm about a performance they had heard the night before and get everybody around the table excited about it.

My father enjoyed doing things with us children, though in those days there was less occasion for it then there is today. I know it was very important to him that we would come along on those endless walks in the woods around our city. He enjoyed holding us by the hand and talking with us, running ahead and teaching new tricks to the dog, Alf, a German Shepherd.

Oh yes, Alf; how could I not have mentioned him before? He was an important member of our family for several years. He was a good-natured, not at all fierce German Shepherd. My father brought him home one day, I don't remember when. He and I became close friends, but I remember that Lisel also was close to him. He sometimes accompanied me to school, and was allowed to return home by himself. I wish I could remember who fed him and what became of him, but I cannot.

When I was about 15 my father yielded to my urgings and taught me to drive. I had been allowed to do the steering for many years, first sitting on his lap and later crunched up next to him. But now he and I would quietly drive off to a lonely stretch of road in the woods somewhere, and he would let me drive. What pleasure—and pleasure, I am sure, not only for me but also for him!

My mother lacked that joy of living, or at least she lacked the ability to express it. She was more self-contained and seldom let her outward dignity lapse. She was much concerned with physical things, like our clothes and our health. She couldn't stand to hear anyone sneeze or cough. Each time we coughed, she would comment on it and want to know why and what we had done to bring it on. I am sure that her feelings were as warm and her concerns at least as deep as those of our father. She simply expressed them differently.

In 1935, that terrible year when my parents finally decided that it was hopeless to try to continue the family business, my father's joie de vivre left him and it really never returned. He became a very serious man, with almost no laughter left in him and he became I would almost say haunted by the decisions which he knew he should be making but couldn't get himself to make. My mother was a strong support in those days and, I suspect, was the one who kept him going. I do recall that they discussed everything endlessly over the dinner table and, I am sure, at other times. They operated very much as a team in those crucial years.

I have alluded several times in this story to the changes which the Nazis' rise to power in Germany would bring. These were subtle changes at first which quickly became direct, brutal and terminal to the way of life I have so far described.

3. NAZI TIMES IN GERMANY

On April 1, 1933, I was then twelve, it all hit home suddenly. It could no longer be ignored or brushed aside as a passing unpleasantness just as soon ignored. That day, when I came home from school, all the display windows of our store, which took up the entire width of our house, had been painted over with black, white and red paint and, in the center, just one enormous word "Jude"—Jew. There were four storm troopers in brown uniforms, two at each entrance, who urged the prospective customers to go away and patronize "German merchants" and to stop buying from Jew-merchants. I remember being with Ida, probably because my parents had sent her to pick me up from school so I wouldn't have to run the gauntlet by myself in order to get into my house. They yelled the then typical expletives for Jews at us like "Scheissjude" or "Stinkjude", shit Jew or stinking Jew, but did not physically prevent us, or anyone else, from entering. Ida, of course, was not at all Jewish, but she loyally stuck it out with us.

The store was virtually empty on that day and on subsequent similar, so-called "Jew boycott" days. There were a few brave souls who braved the rowdies in order to show their disdain, but very, very few. Even the Jewish customers stayed home rather than expose themselves to such abuse and embarrassment. I wish I knew how our employees felt. Most of them probably sympathized with the Nazis, but also didn't want to lose their jobs. There was not a great deal of turn-over among employees in those days. This was their career. Most had been with my family for a long time. I know there was a handful of faithful ones. But most were weather vanes and moved with the wind to their own advantage.

Of course, while this was the day that forced us to begin to face the reality of the aggressive anti-Semitism of the Nazis, it didn't all happen over night. I was not conscious of the existence of such a thing as anti-Semitism until, when I was still quite young, not my class but an upper class in school went as a group to an island in the North Sea. This island was proud to be, and advertised that it was, "judenfrei", i.e. free of Jews. It had maintained this position throughout the 1920s and, I believe, initially uninfluenced by Nazi ideology. It drew its anti-Semitism from deep roots in German nationalism, going back to the Kaiser's Germany and before. Islands such as this catered to aristocrats and other conservatives that had always been anti-Semitic in a social sense, i.e. unwilling to socialize with Jews but not otherwise committed to harming them, let alone to their extinction. I knew some of the Jewish kids who were simply left behind by the school class that went on a visit to that island. They were quite unhappy.

In the early '30s there was a lot of nasty street fighting. Not only the Nazis but also most other parties had their militant militias. The Social Democrats had theirs, the Communists had theirs, and then there were the SA and SS of the Nazis, as well as the very right wing, but not Nazi, Stahlhelm of the German nationalists led by the Prussian Junker families and ex-Army officers. There were lots of street brawls, some of which we observed from our balconies. In school, most of the faculty was quite far to the right, but in the late '20s and early '30s they tended to be fair and did not discriminate against Jews. However, they did make you understand that you were not "one of us", you were something separate and apart. In other words, they were social anti-Semites but of the non-violent sort and, generally, were committed to basic fairness. I do not remember being treated unjustly in those years, though when I failed in gymnastics or missed a goal in soccer, you knew that it was different when a Jew failed or missed than when a non-Jew did. There was sort of a sense of "well, what do you expect of a Jew" in the air. I suppose we got used to it. Honestly, I do not remember it as terribly offensive, although you would think that children would suffer from any sense of apartness from their peers. Other children may well have suffered more.

My parents and most of their friends considered themselves as Germans of Jewish religion. My father and virtually every other man of his generation had served in the German army in World War I. German history and German language, as well as German literature, were important and dear to them. When they traveled abroad, they felt as Germans. At home they spoke French to each other only when they didn't want us children to understand. This happened more and more as the Nazis tightened their grip.

On the high holidays, my parents, like most of our friends, went to the synagogue. My father wore a black suit and his high silk hat on those days and my mother, too, dressed in Sunday clothes. Though we were not so religious as to eat kosher or to refrain from driving on Saturdays, we did not drive to the synagogue. One walked. The synagogue was located on the lower end, in the old city, of our street, a fifteen minute walk from our house. On the high holidays, there was a migration of dressed-up Jews walking decorously with their families to the synagogue, prayer book in hand. As we passed friends and acquaintances, my father would dip his hat, as was expected of gentlemen then. I would do the same with my school cap. There was a lot of mutual hat dipping. I have a sense that non-Jews often came out to watch this migration, but I remember it in those early days as a friendly crowd and as feeling quite proud that I was part of this procession from and to the synagogue. There was none of the wish for obscurity that intruded later.

My father had a seat in the synagogue that he had inherited from his father. All our friends had these seats that had been passed from generation to generation. Of course, that was only true for the men, who were downstairs. The women were segregated in the galleries upstairs, but we could see each other for my mother, too, had a seat of her own in a front row. In the synagogue, my father exchanged his silk top hat for a yarmulke and put on his prayer shawl. He, like everybody else, was familiar with many of the Hebrew prayers, but by sound only. Nobody could understand a word of Hebrew in the sense that they could interpret it into German as it was spoken. One knew the words phonetically and the music—beautiful music that became very familiar—that went with it. If you wanted to know what it meant, you could read the German text on the opposite page of the prayer book.

These whole days in the synagogue on the high holidays were a bore to me and to most of the children I knew. But we did what was expected of us and in the course of it absorbed phonetically the same sounds and music that our parents had absorbed. They are still in my subconscious. Much, much later, when I came to America, I found that the Jewish tradition here has different roots and that both the pronunciation of the Hebrew and, more importantly, the music are different. I found that alienating and disturbing, particularly when, as was true in our case, it was only the sound and the music that had any meaning to us. The words themselves were meaningless, I am sorry to say.

On Yom Kippur my parents fasted from sundown the night before to sundown on Yom Kippur. We went to the synagogue the night before and all day on the high holiday itself. We children were instructed not to fast, but in a way it was a sport and we wanted to be part of it. So most of the time at least as young teenagers, we did the same, not out of any real belief but as a challenge. The evening meal after Yom Kippur was a very special and festive one. The belief was that it was unhealthy to start eating just anything. Therefore, when we came home, only cold pickled herring was served with dry bread. Usually there were friends and family there to celebrate with us "das Anbeissen", the first meal after the fast. Then there was an hour's wait during which there was usually talk and some music. And then a full meal was served and heartily indulged in. I remember some of these as fun evenings with a sense of accomplishment all around.

During the rest of the year, we did little that was related to Judaism, except that on the anniversaries of my grandfather's death, "Jahrzeit", a candle was lit at sundown the night before and my father went to the synagogue to say the Kaddish. He also went to the synagogue on the morning of Jahrzeit.

As I said before, my parents considered themselves Germans in every way and thought that their religion, Judaism, should be looked at as no different than their neighbors' Protestantism or Catholicism. They were, of course, aware of social anti-Semitism but they also knew that it was lessening and had hopes that seemed reasonable to them at that time that it would gradually fade away with the more general acceptance of the democratic ideals and liberalism of the Weimar Republic. Who knows, but for Hitler and the Depression, they might well have been right.

It is important to understand this background in order to try to comprehend, if not accept, the absolute refusal of most of the people in my parent's circle to take the Nazis seriously until it was too late. The thought of leaving Germany as emigrants was simply incomprehensible to them. Our families had been in Germany for hundreds of years, much longer than any Jews of today have been in America. German Jews had their ups and downs in terms of the degree of acceptance by the outside world. That was understandable to them. A swing against the Jews in German politics was regrettable but, looked at historically, not too surprising and, hopefully, a passing phase in a longer term trend towards acceptance and assimilation. This attitude turned out to have been disastrously wrong, of course, but it is important to try to understand it in the context of their backgrounds. I do.

As we moved into the '30s, the Nazis became more prominent in the school. Many of my classmates became members of the Hitler Youth. The youngest of the Hitler Youth were called "Jungvolk". They wore black corduroy shorts, very, very short, the shorter the better. They wore brown shirts with a black kerchief held together by a Nazi swastika ring at the neck. They wore wide military belts with a shoulder strap across one shoulder. Much of what they did was boy scout stuff, with some military drill mixed in. There was also a lot of indoctrination concerning the superiority of the Aryan race. On the whole, however, as children wanting not to be different from their peers, we admired and, since we couldn't joint them, imitated them to the extent we could. I, too, wore very short corduroy pants with knee socks. My military belt had a more neutral buckle than the Jungvolk's swastika. But I have little doubt that, had we been allowed to join, as children we would have. These young people's anti-Semitism was, on the whole, good natured, at least towards me. They made some fun of me, occasionally treated me as an outsider. But for quite a long time they were not unkind. All that changed for the worse as 1933 approached and passed. It became mandatory for us, at the beginning of each hour in school, when the teacher arrived to stand up and greet him with a raised right arm and "Heil Hitler". The Jews—there were six of us in a class of about 25—stood up but raised no arm and kept our mouths shut. More and more we were excluded from activities. Soccer games took place but they no longer allowed Jews to participate. We were so informed by the teacher in advance and asked to stay home. There were no apologies; that's the way it was. One took one's instructions and carried them out.

The swimming clubs along the river became "Judenfrei", free of Jews, and we were expelled from membership by a businesslike notice, containing neither nastiness nor apology. The boat house where my kayak was parked decided that it no longer wished to harbor Jewish-owned kayaks. So that pleasure went overboard. Bicycling alone for me became more risky. Every now and then a small pack of Hitler Youth might attack and beat you up. Our parents began to keep us closer to home. The endless round of birthday parties came to an end. Jews were no longer invited to non-Jewish birthday parties. People in the street, neighbors of many decades, suddenly began to look away. They no longer knew you. It gradually became known which stores would continue to serve you—i.e. were willing to accept your money—and which stores were too unpleasant to patronize.

I can appreciate only in retrospect how terrible these times must have been for my parents, as parents. We all dote on our children. We are all delighted to see them succeed in school, to be popular, to do well in sports, theatrics and be accepted by their communities as valuable contributing members. Our parents must have been just the same, but then everything went wrong. Not only they, but even worse their children became outcasts. The children's peers, so important to growing children, no longer accepted them. Even the doctor's wife who had given me my weekly violin lessons for many years, had begun to greet me with "Heil Hitler" when I, a lone teenager, entered her room . There was no one else there. It could only have been intended to make me as uncomfortable as possible, but still take our money. Eventually my parents must have realized this and those lessons stopped and my father took over.

And our family business, so much the focus of my parents' lives, very quickly went dead. A large retail store, empty, with lots of personnel standing around with nothing to do, is a depressing thing, and I remember it as such. Even as a teenager I felt it hard to walk through the place. Most people simply stopped coming. I do not think it was possible to lay off personnel. In a matter of months a business that had been profitable and growing for almost seventy-five years turned into a losing proposition. My father was very depressed. My parents had endless discussions which we children were not supposed to hear. I suppose they were talking about whether to close the store or try to sell it, or about the latest insults from people who used to be friendly and used to profit from their association with us, or even the possibility of emigration. They tried to save us as much of the pain as possible. There was much talk in French across the dinner table.

Naturally, the people who had been buying at our store or at the big department store down the street or at other Jewish-owned stores had to go other places to shop. So the non-Jewish retailers flourished and found that Nazism and discrimination worked in their favor. They bought it, if they weren't already emotionally carried away by it.

The merchant class and the professionals, as I recall, were the worst. The aristocracy, the ex Army officers, the very rich like the Henschel family, didn't like the rabble rousing and vulgar aspects of national socialism and used an occasional shopping trip to a Jewish store as a way to protest their social and intellectual superiority. My parents talked about some of the "von's" who came in and made a show of it by driving up ostentatiously. Not only could one not make a living off these few demonstrative visits, they also did not last. The buildup of the German army soon won over many of these people. If they or their children did not reenter the army as officers, they liked the German nationalism, the recapture of the Saar territory and the remilitarization of the Rhineland. And as for the Henschels, they began to make tanks. That was more important than demonstrative visits to Jewish stores which, I suspect, in any case were not so much demonstrations in favor of the Jews as demonstrations of their own sense of separateness from the common rabble in the storm troops of the Nazi Party.

As you would expect, under this pressure from outside families like ours became more Jewish. We began to observe the Friday night ceremony of saying Kiddush over bread and wine. It became a social occasion, for which grandmothers and other friends were invited. The headquarters of the Jewish congregation in Kassel became a social center and it organized its own activities for children from pre-schoolers to teenagers. As the opera and theaters became off limits to Jews, the Jewish "Kulturbund", the Culture Association, put on high quality lectures and performances. They did not lack performers. As the big orchestras and stages were cleansed of Jews, their quality went down and the quality of Kulturbund activities went up.

As a teenager, between twelve and fifteen I saw less and less of my classmates outside class hours. In a class of between 30 and 40, there were six Jewish kids. They put up with us in class but would stare past us, not know us, when we met in the street. The same was true for neighbors' kids. The groups that I had been skiing with since I was seven years old would no longer take me. The lady who had organized and lead these trips for years, the wife of the owner of the city's largest wallpaper store and a long-time business acquaintance and neighbor of our family, called my parents to say that she no longer wanted me along. My social life began to center around Jewish organizations. It must have been a wrenching change, but I cannot say that I remember great personal suffering as a result. Perhaps I am blocking it out. Perhaps my personality even then made it easier for me than for most other kids to adapt. Surely lots of Jewish kids like me suffered greatly and were lastingly affected in their self-image and in other ways by being made outcasts in their formative years.

The fact is that I made good, new Jewish friends and we managed to create a social life for ourselves which was satisfying and even included quite a lot of fun. We had a Jewish scout-like organization which went on similar outings as those of the Hitler Youth. We had to be a little careful as to where we went but, on the whole, there was little violence against Jews at that time. It was all done by words—a lot of ridicule—and legal edicts of exclusions. We Jewish teenagers had no hesitancy to stand in the street, as other teenagers did, in groups kidding around with each other and flirting. As other teenagers passed they would make obscene gestures, hold their noses or that sort of thing, but not attack us. We became oblivious to that kind of treatment, though at some level it must have hurt a lot. The strange thing is that I remember the fun we had much more than any such hurts.

I do remember that going to the synagogue on the high holidays now changed from the pleasurable old ceremony to an ordeal, but an ordeal which everybody felt they had to go through. The high silk hats were no longer worn. One dressed as unobtrusively as possible. But the migration to the synagogue still took place, only few, if any, men's hats were tipped. The non-Jews that passed did not wish to be recognized by us.

Between 1933 and 1937 there was little physical violence directed at Jews in Kassel, at least not against Jews who had not been politically active in an overtly anti-Nazi way. That came later. Because life and limb seemed safe and there was an ample financial cushion to absorb economic adversity, a bunker psychology was possible and was adopted. Jews' social life began to center around their own organizations and "they waited things out". Of course there were others who were either smarter or were so heavily involved politically that they did fear early on for their lives. They left. They were the lucky ones who not only left before it was too late but were also able to take a substantial portion of their possessions.

At least two of my parents' friends were not satisfied to wait things out passively. Uncle Victor Oppenheim and my father's closest friend in Berlin, Ludwig Schoeneberg, were smart and courageous enough to begin quietly to transfer assets abroad and nurturing foreign business connections. This involved taking very serious risks, but they were personalities attuned to risk. My parents and most others like them were not. Being law abiding was deeply ingrained. Violating laws prohibiting smuggling property abroad or starting businesses unreported in Germany was foreign to their nature.

In 1935 or 36 my parents decided that my sister Lisel should not continue in the German schools. Perhaps she was the more sensitive of the two of us. I do not know all the reasons, but she was sent away to go to a boarding school in Northern Italy, that part of Italy that was Austrian before World War I. This school on the Vigiljoch—by then Monte San Vigilio—located between Bolzano and Merano, was started by a German Jewish educator who had lost her job in education in Hamburg and was run by her and her husband for kids like us. It was located on a mountain plateau reached by cable car or a long steep hike. Lisel enjoyed being there and made lifelong friends of the couple that ran the school, Miecke and Gotthard Guenther. They. too, ultimately ended up in America and Lisel reestablished contact with them there. She has told me that it was Dr. Gotthard Guenther's influence that caused her to major in philosophy in college.

Lisel 1935

Once again, as I think back, it strikes me how hard it must have been for my parents to part with a thirteen year old daughter, particularly in circumstances where the family's future was so much up in the air. Sending kids away to boarding school was not at all part of our culture. It wasn't done, unless you had an unmanageable child. That made it all the harder, I am sure.

As soon as school was over for me in the summer of 1935, my parents and I traveled to the Tyrol to visit Lisel, and they left me at that same school for the summer. The physical plant consisted of a series of mountain chalets. Amidst a very sporting atmosphere academic standards were also kept very high. In other words, studies were very important, but so was mountain climbing in the Summer and skiing in the Winter. I greatly enjoyed this summer visit. I remember it as a great vacation, with lots of hiking in that beautiful mountain country, swimming and fun with nice kids of similar interests and backgrounds as mine.

In the following summer of 1936, on the other hand, they sent me to a fancy boarding school near Nyon on Lake Geneva, where I was not nearly as happy. For one thing, the going language was French. While I knew quite a bit of school French by then and had no trouble understanding and making myself understood, I was far from fluent when I arrived, which hampered my style. Also, contrary to the Viviljoch, there were no girls; it was an all-boys school. That greatly reduced the fun for me by then. Finally, most of the others were rich kids mostly from England and America, who were sent there to learn French. They tended to be jocks with few interests other than sports and girls, the latter only for talking about because there were no live girls. I remember mostly long bicycle trips up and down the Swiss mountains. That stay did make me quite fluent in French, and now that I think back I believe I was there longer than just for the summer vacation. I think I stayed well into the Fall and I believe the reason for that was that my class at the Gymnasium in Kassel was doing something that Fall from which Jews were excluded. It may have been a special program in a place like Norderney on the North Sea, where Jews were not admitted.

Two years after the boycott of Jewish businesses started, it became clear even to my father that he could not continue in business. Losses began to make alarming inroads in the firm's capitalization and the family's wealth. He began negotiations for the sale of the business. It must have been an excruciatingly difficult decision for him. This wasn't just any business. He had inherited it from his father and I am sure he had expected in typically German fashion to leave it to me. Once it was sold, it was gone. Yet, one still hoped that the craziness of the Hitler times would run its course and change into something better. As a result, there was another compromise. He decided to try to sell the business but keep the real estate, offering a new owner a long term lease, but still only a lease. It left open the possibility that someday the Loeser family might rebuild the business.

Many Jewish businesses at that time were "sold" to people with close Nazi party ties, who used direct duress to force a sale under conditions equivalent to confiscation. My father managed to avoid that specter by selling to the owner of a similar but smaller retail operation in Westphalia, whom he knew. His name was Karlheinz Wiese. He was a conservative Catholic who, we thought, in his heart of hearts disapproved of the Nazis and their tactics. Yet, he was willing and eager to profit by what was happening. He probably said to himself: "If I don't do it, someone else will. So I might as well do it and treat the Jew as fairly as possible." In a way he did. He had all the bargaining chips on his side but he paid full book value for the inventory. That was all there was, of course. The seventy-five year old business and the name "Ferdinand Löser & Company" no longer carried any goodwill in Nazi Germany. And he agreed to pay a fair rent for the business premises to the owner of the building, my father. He did not, like many others in those days, use the threat of imprisonment or bodily harm to get the Jewish property they coveted for next to nothing.

Mr. Wiese did everything politely and according to law. However, he knew well that he was getting an enormous bargain thanks to the Nazis. The day he reopened the doors of the store under his "Aryan" name, the customers flooded back in. He suddenly owned a going business much larger than his original store, all for the cost price of the inventory. I wonder whether he lost any sleep over this injustice. I think it is possible. In fact he almost certainly did five years later when the entire store was bombed to pieces by the RAF, and when the restitution laws of the post-War period forced him to return the real estate to the Loesers. More about that later.

Our bombed out house with
the WIESE sign that used
to say LÖSER, 1945

Another man did lose a lot of sleep observing from close by the revival of the business overnight, just by a change in name and ownership. For my father, I know in retrospect, it was the beginning of the end of his life. His inner self never recovered from that loss, perhaps felt by him as the loss of the fruit of his father's life's work, as well as of his own and his family's secure future.

I had lived through the atmosphere of doom that had prevailed in our apartment for weeks during the negotiations with Mr. Wiese and the preceding period full of agonizing choices. My mother was often in tears—I had seen her tears before—but the day the contract was signed was one of the few times in my life when I saw my father cry. The sad climax came in November 1935 when the sale became effective. I was there and watched as the large vertical sign spelling "Löser" in blue neon letters—a sign that had been visible from afar and had cast a blue sheen into my room every evening as long as I could remember—was taken down and the new name, WIESE, was substituted. Virtually overnight the store was full of customers again.

We were going to continue to live in our duplex apartment above the store we no longer owned—an utterly untenable arrangement, as seems obvious with hindsight. Yet it must have seemed possible to my parents in their then frame of mind. Lisel, away in Italy, missed most of those miserable days, though she surely sensed it and must have seen some of it because she did return to Kassel on vacation every now and then.

The trauma caused by the sale of the store, particularly to my father, may seem exaggerated and unnatural in our age when it is accepted as ordinary for people to change jobs frequently, to move from one coast to another 3000 miles away, and when selling one business and starting another is honored as entrepreneurship. Obviously this was different, because it was done under duress. But there was more to it. Ours was the very opposite of a mobile society. Businesses such as ours were a part of the family, indeed a central part. Ferdinand Löser & Co was not even incorporated. Personal liability was taken for granted. The business was a personal, inherited responsibility and it was expected to stay in the family. No matter that the objective blame for being forced to sell it obviously rested with the Nazis, I believe that the sale caused a strong sense of personal failure in my father, no matter how irrational.

A word about our household employees. Ida stuck with us through thick and thin, as I have mentioned. Of course, as I mentioned earlier, she had left us in what must have been late 1933 or early 1934 after she got married. Yet she visited us regularly and we continued to visit her and her family. She suffered through this period with us. There also continued to be a loyal cook. I have no idea whether it was the red-haired Elise or someone else.

I have previously mentioned Reinecke's toy store, Metzger's leather goods store and the pastry shop across the street from us. The owners all lived, like we, in apartments above their businesses. They had been good neighbors and friends for as long as I can remember. We bought in each others' stores and exchanged almost daily greetings as a matter of course and their children and we shared birthday parties and played in each other's houses. All that stopped by late 1934 and early 1935. Suddenly they looked the other way when we met in the street, all joint partying ceased, and though they continued to be willing to take our money when we came to their shops, we were treated as unwelcome strangers and soon stopped going. These were not people who had been early Nazis or, as far as we knew, had any strong political convictions one way or another. They knew us and our family well enough to understand that the horror stories about Jews in the daily press just could not be true as to us. They were not violent, yet they readily played along with the way the wind blew and, almost without exception, with a pitiless rudeness meant to hurt. Within a year or two most of them would also profit financially from the elimination of virtually all Jewish-owned businesses in Kassel. From that attitude it was only a relatively small step further to look on in silence as their Jewish neighbors, in many cases neighbors of the same families for over a hundred years, were forcibly taken away and shipped east.

German school years then ran from Easter to Easter. Easter 1937 I would finish 10th grade, "das Einjaehrige", the point which I mentioned before at which those kids left high school who did not intend to go on to university. There was no thought of a Jew continuing into the 11th, 12th and 13th grades, which in German schools of those days were strictly university preparatory. The universities were closed to Jews anyway. So my parents had to think of what to do with me. The daughter of close friends, Lotte Oppenheim (her father was the brother of Victor Oppenheim, my father's sister's husband; he was a lawyer with offices opposite us on the Ober Koenigstrasse and he was, of course, my father's lawyer) had gone to a boarding school near Haslemere in Surrey, England, which, like my sister's school in Italy, had been newly founded for refugee children. She spoke glowingly about the school when she came home on vacations. My parents decided to send me to that school. That meant that at Easter 1937 I would leave Germany, and I knew about it well in advance.

I've been trying to remember what I thought about this prospective big change in my life. I was much unhappier about it than I let on to my parents. I was, by then, a teenager much involved in hanging out with other kids. Girls had become important. I was sad about having to leave my friends. We had a group of Jewish teenagers that had grown close to each other and we managed to have lots of fun notwithstanding what was going on around us. But I was particularly upset by the notion that in a foreign country speaking another language I would be unable to reestablish such relationships. The word plays that were part of kidding around with your friends were important. I had always been a good student in German and a good writer of essays. I was not particularly good in foreign languages. I didn't think I could possibly become as fluent and as glib in another language as I felt I was in German. I remember knowingly and consciously grieving over that, in fact crying over it in my bed at night. I found the impending loss of my language and the associated culture more scary than leaving my parents and friends. There was, of course, also some excitement attached to this idea of a major change, but leaving German culture and everything it meant to me came very hard and, in some ways, seemed inconceivable. When our teenage group met and I made a quick and amusing repartee in response to something a friend had said, it would suddenly strike me that I might never again shine in this way, for how could one possibly do that in another language? I had had less than two years of English in school, I knew very little and didn't like what little I did know. French had come more easily because of my firm foundation in Latin. I remember that Winter of 1936 to 1937 as a lot of fun with intense though shifting boy/girl relationships, but tinged with a lot of sadness and finality as well. There was a melancholy aspect to our gaiety.

German Jews had distinguished themselves in commerce, the professions, the arts and the like. These were the expectations which people like my parents had for their children. Probably I would follow my father in the business, but if instead I had chosen to be a lawyer or a doctor or a professor, that would have been regrettable but ultimately acceptable. Now, suddenly, these expectations were shattered. As a consequence my parents and their peers decided that their children could not possibly make it abroad in business or the professions. They had heard that doctors, lawyers and businessmen who had emigrated considered themselves lucky to find work as day laborers. Their children, they thought, would be better off if they became farmers or learned a trade. The common wisdom was that a good carpenter or plumber will always be able to get a job, be it in Argentina or Brazil or South Africa or the United States—the countries most often mentioned for immigration. Therefore, the trend was to try to apprentice your children early to someone who could teach them a trade. The Wertheim family, related to my mother, had a large factory of some sort—I really don't remember what they made—in Frankfurt, and that factory included a carpentry shop. During one of my vacations in 1936 I was apprenticed to a carpenter at that factory, and lived with relatives who were part of the family that owned the plant. I did my best, but I don't think I was very enthusiastic. Anyway, after about two weeks, a chisel slipped and ended up deep in my left hand. The scar is still there. It required all kinds of stitching, and it also put an end to my training as a carpenter.

Recently, when we found old brochures from the early days of Stoatley Rough School in England, the school that I was to be sent to in the Spring of 1937, we discovered that very much the same philosophy prevailed among the founders of that school. Women should learn household and child caring skills so that they could become maids and nannies, and boys should learn to become farmers. Only the occasional child who was unusually gifted was to take the academic route. In practice, things worked out very differently, although some kids, quite a number in fact, were adversely affected by that philosophy. More about that later.

I left for England with my violin under my arm at Easter 1937. I will come back to what followed in another chapter. My parents must have sent me off with a very, very heavy heart. By that time they realized that the finality of the sale of the business was only the beginning of an entirely new phase in their lives. They began to understand that living on top of a business that used to be yours was one of the worst locations for finding a new basis for life. My father, with nothing to do, must have been in a terrible state. Now the last of their children was going off to a life which they expected to be extremely difficult and unlikely to offer a promising future. Yet my parents stayed on, driven by indecision and uncertainty, until an event occurred that, like the boycott of Jewish businesses a few years earlier, forced their hands.

The Nazi were obsessed with race and the purity of the Aryan race. Therefore, they looked upon sexual intercourse between Jews and Gentiles as a great sin. It was called "Rassenschande", literally "the shame to the race" but really connoting the "dirtying" of the race. It was made a crime. Jews found guilty of it were often physically attacked, incarcerated and never again seen.

This reminds me of something else that is relevant at this point in the story. The Nazis rather cleverly gave a lot of support to a pornographer from Nurnberg who specialized in pornographically picturing Jews as rapists and preoccupied with sexual crimes against Aryans. They subsidized his weekly newspaper called *Der Stuermer*, which specialized in the rawest kind of anti-Semitism. Most of the stories and pictures had sexual connotations, and that is why the Nazi propaganda machine cleverly supported it. Then, as now, sexual news attracts attention and is read by people. The spicy sex in *Der Stuermer* made people read the newspaper and thereby absorb the horrors, mostly sexual, imputed to Jews in *Der Stuermer*. There were display cases all over German cities where copies of *Der Stuermer* were shown in such a way that passers-by could stop and read them through the glass. Because of the sexy contents, virtually all young people did, and many older ones as well. There used to be crowds in front of those displays waiting for a chance to read. Even I, a Jewish teenager, couldn't quite abstain from reading those spicy stories occasionally, though it was embarrassing for a Jew to be seen stopping there.

I give this background because it is important to note that there was quite an important sexual connotation to Nazi anti-Jewish propaganda, and the event that gave impetus to my parents' leaving Kassel was related to this aspect of Nazism.

My father was accused of "Rassenschande" with a German woman who was a department head in our store, Fraulein Noedig. I remember her quite well. She had been a loyal employee for a long time. Apparently, she was observed with my father in our car in a secluded place in one of the forest areas around Kassel, and that was enough. There were rumors of charges about to be brought, of imminent arrest. This, at long last, triggered my parents into action. They left Kassel in a hurry and moved to Berlin. The charges were not pursued once my parents had gone from Kassel. I don't know the details of how this was accomplished. I was, of course, no longer with them at this point.

What was the true story? Obviously, I don't know all. What is clear is that after the sale of the store and while continuing to live in the same house my father was fanatically—and, I am afraid, pathetically—interested in what was happening in the business and how the new people were managing. Fraulein Noedig, who continued as a department head under the new owners, was able, and loyal enough to be willing, to give him that information. So he periodically took her out to pump her for news and details of the store. Given the circumstances, particularly her obvious interest in not being observed with my father, they had to do their talking in out-of-the-way places. That far I am sure the story is correct. Whether anything else went on between them on these trips I don't know. I doubt it.

This event was, of course, an enormous shock to my mother and father, and to all of their friends and acquaintances in Kassel. I think it was the first time that they began to realize that staying on in Germany could put their lives in danger. Yet all they were galvanized into doing was to move to the relative anonymity of Berlin and settle there in a nice, very comfortable apartment on the Jenaer Strasse in Berlin-Wilmersdorf. They could have moved into a hotel while preparing their emigration as quickly as possible. My father in 1937 was only 51 years old and my mother four years younger. They could not have been resigned to living out their lives quietly and incognito in a big city such as Berlin while hoping that their children could make new and better lives for themselves abroad. Perhaps they still had the secret hope that all this madness would blow over. Whatever the reason, we know that they took no more than the minimum step necessary to preserve their existence.

I had left for England at Easter 1937 and Lisel was still in Italy. The event that finally drove my parents from Kassel to Berlin must have occurred that Fall, for I returned once more to Kassel on vacation that summer, but spent part of the 1937 Christmas vacation with my parents in Berlin. At that time, there was much talk about emigration. Let me describe the problem that faced people like my parents. I was seventeen then and my parents not only discussed these matters freely with me but also had me come along when it was discussed with lawyers and other friends and advisers.

These friends included the lawyer, Joseph Kaskell, who was to play an important role in my later life, in that it was he who persuaded me to apply to law schools in 1946. I met him for the first time at a dinner that winter at a well known restaurant on the Wannsee, the big lake in the outskirts of Berlin. The main topic of conversation was what countries to consider for emigration and how to get property out of Germany. Places like that large restaurant on the Wannsee were chosen, I believe, because these large institutions provided the greatest degree of anonymity. One was never sure whether a smaller place would look closely at you, identify you as Jews and chase you out.

Another adviser who was often consulted was my father's old friend, Ludwig Schoeneberg, who had a large, well known retail store in the center of Berlin and was extremely savvy in international matters. He was one of the few who managed to get most of his property out of Germany, illegally of course, and, like Victor Oppenheim, also managed to get that rarest of permissions, the permission to settle permanently in Switzerland. I remember his beautiful villa in Kladow, overlooking one of the lakes outside Berlin.

At this time, the Schoeneberg villa was a sad place because we all knew that before long he would have to give it up. But as I write this I remember a much earlier, happier visit to that place where I, as a much smaller boy, was enormously impressed because there, for the first time in my life, I saw a gadget that is taken for granted in virtually every house and apartment these days but that was then a far out extravagance. I refer to a thermostat regulating the heating system. He had one of those newfangled devices in his villa. Virtually every other place, including our house in Kassel, had a large coal fired furnace in the basement which sent steam pulsating through radiators all over the building. It kept on firing away down there, no matter what the need was for heat. Regulation in the rooms took place by turning radiators off and on. However, now that I have said this, I also remember my father going down to the basement on very cold days and pulling chains that opened doors to increase the draft and make it hotter. There may have been other times when he did the opposite due to unexpectedly warm weather. The furnace was tended, of course, by a janitor who was paid to shovel coal into it and regulate it day and night.

To get back to the emigration problems that were the subject of discussion at these meetings: Germany, contrary to Russia and other dictator-ruled countries later on, did not generally close its borders to Jews and others who wanted to leave. What it did was to restrict what they could take along. If you wanted to leave badly enough, you could get on a train with ten marks in your pocket and go—that is if you had a country that would let you in. Therefore, the problems that faced emigrants like my parents were, first, what countries would receive them and, second, how much of their property they could take along to help give them a start in a strange place.

As to destinations, there were none that would receive you readily and with open arms. All of the western democracies had strict immigration laws that regulated how many and who could come. England and France had let in quite a few German refugees in the early Nazi years, but by 1937/38 they had pretty well closed down. There were some exceptions when you had local sponsors and connections, or family members, already in the country; but that was just about it. Later on and to its everlasting credit, England made generous exceptions for children by themselves. More about that later in this history. The United States had numerical quotas, but anti-Semites in the State Department and in Congress succeeded in greatly restricting the availability of visas for German and Austrian Jews. Therefore, there were long waiting lists. In addition, you could only get a quota visa if you had an affidavit from a financially capable resident of the United States to the effect that he or she would be responsible for you and undertook to guarantee that you would not become a public burden. Therefore, to go to the United States, a long wait was inevitable and, in addition, it could only be done through a connection with someone willing and able to give the all-important affidavit. South Africa, Argentina and Brazil had more relaxed attitudes. I don't remember the details but I do remember that it was possible to go to those countries after a wait, and sometimes also to other South American countries such as Chile and Peru.

And then there was Palestine. My parents were not Zionists. That followed from their commitment to German citizenship. Zionists, whose adherents greatly increased after 1933 in Germany, wanted to go to Palestine but could not because of the exclusionary regulations imposed by the British as the mandated power. There, too, a local supporter or local property ownership was required to qualify for an immigration visa. In short, every destination posed its problems. There were endless paperwork and bureaucratic frustrations. It was difficult to decide which way to move, particularly if one's first choice—say, the United States—imposed delays and conditions which it was unclear whether one could fulfill them and when. Should one wait for the first choice or go elsewhere? The paper work and conflicting advice and rumors piled up. In sum, the nature of the obstacles was such as to invite procrastination—unfortunately fatal procrastination for many.

The second problem was property. For people like my parents it was difficult, perhaps almost impossible, to imagine what life without any financial reserves would be like, let alone such a life in a strange country with a foreign language. The German rules for taking property along had tightened up year by year. By 1937/38, when I first became familiar with them, they were something like this: first, an emigrant had to pay a tax equivalent to 50% of the value of everything he owned. Ironically, this tax was called the flight-from-the-country tax, "die Reichsfluchtsteuer". The remaining 50% tended to include all the illiquid assets and out of it funds also had to be set aside to guarantee the payment of real and trumped up debts and for taxes on the liquidation of assets and other imposts on emigrants. What remained could be transferred abroad through bank channels but at rates set by the German government at a confiscatory level. By 1938 the exchange rate for Jews had dropped to perhaps 9% of the standard exchange rates. In short, almost everything was confiscated, though with typical German bureaucratic correctness, the word "confiscation" never entered into the process, it was all done by duly enacted taxes and other imposts. In the end one then estimated that something like 3% of what a person owned might be realized abroad in the currency of the new country.

Furniture and personal belongings could be taken along, subject to some exclusions. All who had money bought clothing sufficient to last for years. Leica cameras became treasures because they might be saleable abroad. It was also possible to pay for the tickets for anticipated travel abroad in pre-tax German marks. And then, naturally, there were illegal routes for getting money out, and after all, what is "illegal" when you deal with unconscionably inequitable and discriminatory laws? Yet that distinction did not come easily to people like my parents.

Others had no trouble with it. I know of friends of my parents who on trips to Switzerland found ways to hide large amounts of money and other valuables in the washrooms of cross-border trains, to be recovered on the other side if all went well. There were American and other foreign sharp operators in Germany then who had use for German Marks and were willing to make deals with Jews, accepting their Marks in return for promises to reimburse the Jews when they arrived abroad—with a large discount, of course. How could one know whether these people would keep their promises? They might disappear or they might even, once they had your money, denounce you to the Nazis so as to get you off their backs with finality. Illegal currency transactions were punishable by death. There were known precedents for such treachery, but also for honest deals.

All these and many others constituted the kinds of possibilities and risks that my parents discussed and weighed endlessly with their friends and advisors in my presence that winter in Berlin. After I returned to England they continued spending most of their waking hours exploring and worrying about these types of problems, the pros and cons of this and that, meeting with various people who offered one or another opportunity—and yet doing nothing. At some time during this period they sold the house in Kassel to Mr Wiese, who probably had a right of first refusal. Mr Wiese, correct as ever and profit-wise as ever, paid the assessed value. Market value was in another ballpark, but one closed to Jews. This transaction again caused endless paper work, taxes to be negotiated and claims to be settled. More reason, I am afraid, for keeping busy and not cutting the cord.

Sadly, this process continued until "Kristallnacht" on November 9, 1938. That is the night when the synagogues all over Germany were set on fire by carefully organized Nazi gangs. It is also the night on which large numbers of Jewish men, particularly men of means, were arrested and shipped to one of several concentration camps, a new German invention. My father, too, was arrested that night and shipped to the concentration camp Dachau near Munich.

Once again, an outside event instigated by the Nazis against my father electrified my parents—in this case, my mother—into action. Within six weeks she managed to get my father out of Dachau on the condition that she and he leave Germany promptly. She spent a great deal of our money to bring about this result. There was corruption in the Nazi hierarchy. She arranged for friends of friends, who lived in Holland to receive them and thus she and my father arrived in Holland in early January 1939 with a couple of suitcases and virtually no money. My mother had managed, however, to liquidate the apartment in Berlin and to have all of its contents, including most of the furniture that had survived the move from Kassel and a lot of valuables which they had accumulated in their attempts to convert German money into goods saleable abroad, into what were then called "Lifts", i.e. container-sized crates. These were left in a storage warehouse in Berlin, subject to being shipped upon later instructions. All other affairs were left in the hands of a lawyer in Berlin, a Jewish man married to a non-Jew, who had decided not to leave Germany come what may. His name was Dr. Sally Engelbert. I remember a huge volume of correspondence with him much later from New York. He did not survive the War.

But how did my mother manage to get the permission to enter Holland, given what I have described concerning other country's immigration laws? The answer is interesting. Many, many years before, when all was well, my father was asked to make a donation to a Jewish development organization in Palestine. I suspect that the request came through my uncle Ludwig, my mother's brother and the only rabid Zionist in that generation of our family, who must have thought that his rich relatives in Germany should help. In any case, my father made a contribution which, as luck would have it, took the legal form of a small ownership interest in an orange grove. I even remember the name of the Palestinian organization, "Hanotaya", probably because there was much correspondence later from New York about selling this interest. However, at the crucial moment in late 1938, it turned out that by reason of this much earlier charitable gift my father was a "property owner" in Palestine and, as such, was entitled to preference in the allocation of visas. So my mother was able to garner an immigration visa for Palestine for her and her husband, and once that was on hand it was easy to get temporary visitors visas for Holland and also England, so that they could visit my sister and me there before departing for Palestine.

My father's plan was to try to establish himself in Palestine. He was not very hopeful about that. He knew that he had none of the skills one was supposed to have to succeed there, such as the ability to run a farm or to work in the building trades. He was prepared to end up driving a taxi or a bus, for he had heard—correctly—that these were well paid professions in that country and, of course, they required qualifications that he had. A realistic appraisal, but not a cheerful prospect for the future. He thought that the opportunities for my sister and me would be much greater in the United States. We were on waiting lists for an American visa, and my father had established contact with a distant cousin who had many decades ago disappeared in the United States but, through a search service, had been located in Philadelphia. He would try to obtain an affidavit of support from him. How difficult and embarrassing it must have been for him to write those begging letters to a person whom we had never helped or cared about when we were well off! It all took its toll on him, I am sure.

Whether the whole family could and would later reunite in the United States, depended on the visa uncertainties, what he could find to do in Palestine, and on whether my parents could arrange after their arrival in Palestine for the forwarding of the lift with the family belongings and, through Dr. Engelbert, for the transfer of what little remained of the family fortune to a Palestinian bank.

My parents lived in Tel Aviv from early 1939 until the end of that eventful year. It was not a happy time for them. My father was preoccupied with endless correspondence with Germany to try to salvage what could be salvaged. One of the interesting things he arranged for, before the final money transfer, was to buy tickets for himself and my mother from Tel Aviv to New York and similar tickets for Lisel and myself from England to New York. This is why, when we finally went, Lisel and I traveled first class on a large Dutch ocean liner, the Statendam.

In Tel Aviv my parents lived pretty much in a German Jewish ghetto. The only people they saw were other refugees from Germany like themselves. They found it impossible to learn Hebrew and, I think, gave it no serious try. They knew some English, which helped them get along in those days of the British Mandate, but they mostly spoke German to fellow refugees. They found the climate extremely hard to adapt to. My father found no basis for building a new existence. Pretty soon the American opportunity loomed larger and larger in their minds. Also, World War II had broken out in September 1939 and the faraway United States seemed a better ultimate destination for both them and their children, if only for physical survival.

Therefore, enormous effort was put into trying to speed up the visa process and to find one or more persons willing to give the vaunted affidavit. "Affidavid", pronounced as a German word and with the name, David, the only recognizable component, became a magic word that every German Jew knew. It was the holy grail of those days. Only years later was I able to figure out that this magic word describing the key to the American gates of entrance was a plain old legal term for a sworn statement.

A black sheep cousin in America, I think his first name was Selmar, turned out to be a banquet waiter in Philadelphia. And though he had never been helped in his own tough existence—I don't really know about that, but I assume that it was such from the profession in which he found himself at an advanced age—he agreed without hesitation to give the required affidavit of support for our entire family. It was a generous and unselfish act by a virtual stranger, which he had every reason to believe could cost him dearly. However, his means were limited and it was thought that his affidavit alone would not be enough. In the meantime, however, Walter Burchard, the son of my father's cousin from

Karlsruhe—the one that he used to telephone with so regularly as reported in Section 1—had settled in New Jersey with his family. He had left Germany early enough to have rescued a portion of his money. He offered to supplement the Philadelphia man's affidavit, and the two together did the trick. In the Fall of 1939 it appeared that a family reunion in New York might be possible. This became the aim.

Accordingly, in the last few months in Palestine my parents sold most of their furniture and belongings, to turn them into cash. How could they have known that their Biedermeier furniture would some day, with the revival of interest in the antecedents of Art Deco, become very valuable in New York, while in Palestine it was plentiful for obvious reasons and, moreover, did not last in that climate? They had more difficult decisions to make at that point, such as what few treasures, family pictures, jewelry, they should drag to New York. There was little money to ship these things, nor any sense that they might be useful in the attempt to build a new existence in America.

Late in 1939 Lisel and I received the tickets for travel on the Dutch liner "Statendam" to New York in late December 1939. By that time, slow ships traveled in convoy, but our fast liner was presumed to be safe from the danger of U-boat attack during this "phony war" period and we traveled on our own. On one of the first days of 1940, the Statendam docked at a West Side pier in Manhattan. We were picked up by Mrs. Burchard, who informed us that at this very moment our parents' ship was docking in Hoboken and that her husband was picking them up.

Lisel had left Germany in 1935 and I in 1937. Now my parents, who had just barely got out of Germany in one piece in early 1939, and us "children" aged 19 and 17 had arrived in New York City by ship within hours of each other. Later on that cold January day in 1940 our family was reunited in America, in a small furnished flat on 40th Street in Long Island City, which the Burchards had thoughtfully rented for us.

That ends my Germany chapter. I will return to the American story in a later Chapter. First, I want to pick up my story after leaving Kassel for England at Easter 1937.

2

ENGLAND

I left Kassel to continue my education at Stoatley Rough School in England in April 1937. I did so because that is what my parents had decided, not because I wanted to leave Germany and home, but as soon as I got to Stoatley Rough I found that I loved it and it quickly became a new home.

My parents had taken me to Hamburg and after a teary farewell watched me board a train to Bremerhaven, where I boarded the "Hamburg", a large German liner destined for New York with a stop at Southampton. Why this unusual route from Germany to England? I think it was because a German ship could be paid for with German money. Obtaining foreign money had become particularly expensive or impossible for Jews. Perhaps my ticket also included a passage all the way to New York for possible later use.

The first class passage on the "Hamburg" was uneventful. I debarked the next day at Southampton—and I was lost. At my German gymnasium I had had six years of Latin, four of French and only two years of English. I didn't understand a word anybody said upon landing in Southampton, but somehow managed to find the train station and the London train that was scheduled to stop at my destination, Haslemere, Surrey.

At Haslemere I unloaded my baggage, including my violin in a new shock-proof case, and managed to get a taxi to the School. Haslemere taxi drivers had learned by then that people with little or no English had to be taken to Stoatley Rough. .

My taxi drove me up Farnham Lane, bordered by entrances—some of them quite grand—to English country houses. Few houses were actually visible from the street. Stoatley Rough turned out to be the last and largest place, at the end of the Lane. I remember being overwhelmed by the beauty of the wide open view from the terrace into a green valley and gentle rolling hills beyond. Below the terrace was a steep incline with flower beds nearby, trees, a lawn tennis court, a playing field further down and then more trees. The very best of English landscape!

But even stronger in my memory was the pleasure I felt on being greeted so warmly and in German, probably by "Miss Astfalck". Up until that moment I had been utterly confused and unhappy, not only because of my inability to communicate. People also looked and behaved quite differently from what I was used to and most turned away from me uncomprehendingly when I tried to say something to them. God, what a relief to be back in a comfortable German atmosphere. It was the beginning of a wonderful and formative association in my life.

Stoatley Rough School, Haslemere, Surrey 1938

The School had been founded in 1934 for German and Austrian refugee children. A large English country house with many acres of grounds, a lawn tennis court and a resident gardener to take care of the beautiful garden had been made available by an English Quaker family, the Vernons. Operating funds came from both Quaker—and in the most part—Jewish sources. Four German women educators were in charge. Two of them, Dr. Hilde Lion, the headmistress, and Dr. Emmy Wolff, were academicians and intellectuals, who had held leading positions in the German women's and social work movements. They had lost their jobs because they were Jewish and had emigrated. The other two, Nore Astfalck and Hannah Nacken, came from similar backgrounds in the women's movement and social work, but were more practically inclined. They were not Jewish, and voluntarily left Germany to take this job. As the idealistic but practical persons that they were, they understood that helping refugee children might be their most effective protest against what was then happening in Germany.

By 1937 there were perhaps 50 students, boys and girls, at the School. They ranged in age from four to the early twenties. Close to half were not assigned to academic studies, but were "household trainees". They had to help run the school household, clean, work in the kitchen, mend clothes, function as teaching assistants etc. The idea was that they were being trained as eventual household helpers in the homes of wealthy families in whatever country might ultimately admit them permanently. Others, mainly boys, worked on a primitive farm with an agricultural teacher, to become farmers. The then prevailing notion was that the only future for most refugee children lay in practical, non-professional work. In retrospect, this was a well-intentioned but wrong-headed idea. Virtually none of us Stoatley Rough kids settled down as permanent farmers, household helpers or artisans, but many of them were, as a result, deprived of an education that would have been more useful in their later lives.

There were some English teachers and, of course, the very English gardener and a handyman, but everyone else at Stoatley Rough was German. English was the official language, but it was a strange English, not only heavily accented, but also full of phrases either literally translated from the German or a mixture of German and English "Ich will's mal try", for example, meaning "I'll give it a try"; or "I am house today", signifying that I have been assigned to the house cleaning detail for the day.

Upon arrival a student guide showed me through the house and took me to a room known as "The Tin", where I met Klaus Zedner, with whom I was to share that room. What a great setup for two 16-year-old-boys! The room was at the end of a long corridor behind the kitchen and well away from everyone else. It also had its own entrance from the outside. One could slip in and out day and night, unobserved and without having to account to anybody. Over the next few days, as Klaus and I quickly became friends, he briefed me on all essential facts, such as food, teachers and other kids, particularly of course the girls.

In the first few minutes after arrival in The Tin I noticed a trap door in the ceiling. When I asked Klaus about it, it appeared that he had never taken note of it and knew nothing about it. I did not rest that first day until I had explored what lay behind it. It turned out to be a small room under the eaves, connected by a crawl space to the building's attic. It struck me at once as a great potential hideout and partying space. It became just that soon after. We called it the "Klingsburg", "Burg" being German for "castle". The significance of "Klings" must have been great but is now lost in history. More about our "Klingsburg" later.

At some point shortly after my arrival I encountered Dr. Lion for the first time, and we had a private talk. No one had prepared me for her peculiar, nervous "hm's" as she talked which, like most children on first impression, I thought were funny. But I liked her. I have no memory as to what we talked about, but it was the beginning of a very good rapport with her which lasted for as long as we knew each other. It also didn't take long for me to find out that I was one of the favored, privileged ones. She was a strong, commanding woman, of considerable intellectual ability and a driving desire to succeed as well as do good. As time went on, she undertook enormous efforts to help my sister Lisel and myself. We were not the only ones. A good many students owe the beginning of their careers, and in many cases their lives, to her energy and efforts. Though her desire to do well by her students while they were studying as well as after graduation was dominant, she was unfortunately also able to make life hard for those whom she didn't like for some reason or—more often—those whom she had wrongly pigeonholed as, say, potential farmers, or as not suited—or only suited—for academic work. Once one became classified in her mind, it was hard to break out even though the classification didn't fit. Luckily, she had figured me right. I was able to do good academic work, but was also suited to practical life and to applying what I had learned to maximum advantage.

To some extent finances also entered into her calculus. Many thought it should not have to the extent it did, but the School functioned on a financial shoestring and it was her responsibility to make ends meet. Anyway, I was a paying student, because my parents could afford to deliver full tuition in England though this meant forfeiting to German chicanery almost ten times the actual monthly payments. Many other kids at the School were not so lucky.

Whatever the reasons, I was assigned to the academic program leading to Cambridge School Certificate, the certificate then of high school completion. If you did well in that examination, exemption from a further university matriculation test could also be won, known for short as "Matric". However, being in the academic program by no means meant a Groton-type of boarding school life. My bed in The Tin consisted of a board suspended a few inches above the floor with only a very lumpy mattress between it and myself. Except for one or two classrooms, most teaching and studying took place in improvised settings around a round library table or dining room tables, or just sitting in chairs in a circle. In good weather, classes moved outside. In addition, we, like everyone else, had to help in the kitchen, do washing-ups, keep our rooms clean and make our beds, and assignment to many other practical "jobs", as they were known.

Every now and then there was a "Workday". That meant that no classes took place, everyone dressed in work clothes, and each person was assigned to a special detail: cleaning the house from top to bottom; preserving food for future use; repairing clothes; repairing and making needed furniture and fixtures; painting walls, etc. I remember being part of a team that produced a wooden bicycle rack one Workday, and stands calibrated for suspending a high-jump rope (no bars in those days) another time. Workdays were not something most of us moaned about. We liked them. It was fun to work as part of a team, to be free from academic work and to produce useful results. Those days added to the prevailing sense of camaraderie and, since the teachers also pitched in, it brought us closer to them and was a good way to get to know them better. Usually Workdays ended up with a better-than-ordinary meal and then sitting by one of the rare fires in the fireplace, talking and singing.

While Dr. Lion helped engineer my future, Miss-Astfalck-and-Miss-Nacken (a twosome that, as I soon understood, was more than the sum of one plus one) were the personalities that had the greatest influence on me over the next few years and, in many ways, helped shape me as a person. They created a new home for me, as for many others at Stoatley Rough. They were strict and expected much from us, but we knew also that they held themselves to even higher standards. Their sense of responsibility, their confidence that every problem, big or small, could be solved, their sense of fairness and their love of beauty, inspired us to emulate these qualities. Contrary to the headmistress, they could be relied on not to play favorites and, when the chips were down, they were our friends and our advocates.

Of course, there were also down sides to their regime. How can I ever forgive Miss Astfalck for making me get up day after day at an ungodly hour of the morning to go on "The Run", a half hour of calisthenics out in the cold. Porridge for breakfast? Most of us had never seen or heard of such a thing. And it had to be eaten. I actually got to like it, but most of the other kids gagged on it. And then there were those enormous "washing ups" which left one's hands shriveled for hours. But there were many more times when I personally experienced Astfalck/ Nacken's humanity, and willingness to bend the rules in ways that were important to a 16 year old. For example, though we maintained utter secrecy about the many "Night Walks" with others, particularly girls, deep down we sensed that Astfalck/Nacken knew and tolerated within limits this outlet for teenage energy and experimentation. Another example: Klaus and I had furnished our Klingsburg with various old mattresses and pillows and homemade decorations which had transformed this space into a comfortable nest for late night parties, mostly serious talkfests and opportunities to get to know other kids better. Eventually, Miss Astfalck, who missed nothing for long, found out about it. She raised some hell over the unauthorized disappearance of useful things, but she was also pleased with our inventiveness and decorating skills. When we offered a deal, namely that she would be invited to our next Klingsburg party, she accepted—and did come. The extra pleasure of secrecy was now gone, but a new, conspiratorial bond had been established with Miss Astfalck which felt good. It was the beginning of a friendship that lasted for the rest of her long and wonderfully productive life.

Academic work at Stoatley Rough fell into two distinct types in my memory. There was the teaching by those of German background, Dr. Wolff and Dr. Lion, and later Dr. Leven in music. It was comfortable, familiar and wholly understandable, and often inspiring. Then there was the teaching by English instructors. I remember mainly Miss Dove and Col. Hamilton—two opposites in personality and teaching style. Miss Dove was a gentle person in her early twenties, just recently out of teachers training. She never raised her voice but had lots of ways of looking at literature that had never even occurred to me. She was open-minded and did her best to stimulate our imagination. Col. Hamilton was a rigid former Army man of clipped speech, to whom mathematics was a given that one had to learn by heart, but never question. Ideas had nothing to do with it. Just read the book, listen and memorize. What these two so vastly different persons had in common in my memory was that neither realized how fractional our—or at least my—understanding then was of what they were saying. Miss Dove, like many English-speaking people, spoke in a very low voice with relatively little vocal emphasis. One had to listen carefully to each word. No German teacher ever talked that way. My ears were more attuned to listening for the typical pick up in volume to emphasize the important things.

That unaccustomed way of communicating, plus my lack of English vocabulary, often made it difficult for me to follow her thoughts. But I understood very soon that what she had to say was fascinating. I had never had a literature teacher who expressed ideas beyond those in the book and who invited and encouraged that kind of free thinking on our part and digging deep into meanings. The frustration came from my limited ability to understand and to express myself, though that improved in time.

In retrospect it is extraordinary how much of her teaching has stuck with me after all. King Lear, Macbeth and Twelfth Night are still the Shakespeare plays I know best, and the deeper understanding of their meaning which she gave us still resonates in my mind. She also exposed us to English poetry from the Oxford Book of English verse. To this day I remember fractions of Keats' "Ode to a Grecian Urn", scraps of Coleridge's fantastic language of dream-like nonsense and quite a few others. Years later, when I went to City College in New York at night, her teaching, her approach to language and literature, were instrumental in enabling me to deal imaginatively with new material and gave me an understanding that was not only a source of pleasure to me but also resulted in the adequate grades that ultimately, after the War, helped get me into Harvard Law School—the true intellectual watershed in my life.

Col. Hamilton's teaching, to the contrary, gave me no understanding whatsoever of the meaning and uses of mathematics, something I have greatly missed in later life, and still miss. He did, however, get me through Matric math with no trouble—a sad reflection, I am afraid, on the nature of the examination process at the time. He did also teach me examination-taking techniques based mainly on organization, outlining and memory—irrespective of real understanding—which, I must confess, have also stood me in very good stead at various crucial junctures.

What helped greatly was that my "class" for the most important subjects consisted of only two kids, myself and Barbara "Baerbel" Gerstenberg, a girl from Berlin, about my age and from a similar background. In short, our classes were really private tutorials. This concentrated teacher-student relationship forced me never to let my attention lag, as often happened in larger classes when language problems made it hard to keep up. I was lucky once again, and Baerbel and I became close friends in that pressure cooker of one-on-two instruction. We have remained so to this day, though we manage to meet only rarely.

Of course there were many more subjects that we had to prepare for Matric, but I must confess I remember few of the teachers and the classes. We were going to be tested orally as well as in writing in French and German. German was a cinch for us, but preparing to take a French dictation, speaking French to the examiner and writing a French essay called a "précis" took much hard work. Then there was History, a subject I had loved in Germany. The European History portion therefore was relatively easy for me, but English History was another thing. We were supposed to concentrate on the period 1688 to 1914, but what German-trained boy had ever heard of Disraeli or all the kings called James and Charles? That also took hard work, as did English Literature. We were even going to be tested in Geography, a subject then important in all European schools. It was a struggle to bone up on all those subjects in order to take that darn examination in June 1938, only a little over a year after my arrival in England. Although I have good recollection only of Miss Dove's small classes with Baerbel in English Literature and History, and Col. Hamilton in Math, the other teachers must also have done their job well, for I did pass the examination on first try. This was an examination given countrywide at the same time, and I seem to recall that a relatively small percentage of English students managed to pass all subjects the first time around.

Baerbel and I took our Matric at a large examination center, I believe in Guildford, the county seat. That must have been about June 1938. We had a long walk on each of the three days of the examination, down through the garden and then along a footpath, probably to a bus stop. Anyway, we were fond of each other and the long, un-chaperoned walks with her—sometimes even holding hands—made up for the dread of what lay at the end of each morning's hike. I knew that Baerbel knew things ever so much better than I, and could manipulate her knowledge according to her own thoughts, while I was mainly stuffed with well-organized, memorized facts. Compared to her, I thought I should fail, but then, when I saw the English kids who also took the exam, I became more confident that I should be able to do as well as they. My passing that examination has made me suspicious of what that type of examination proves ever since. I not only passed, I made "Matric".

I have many good memories of holiday celebrations at Stoatley Rough. They were warm, participatory events, with lots of home-made decorations and, sometimes, costumes. There was always good music, good even though it sometimes included me in the role of first violinist. I was never very good at it and abandoned my violin when I left Stoatley Rough—regretfully in retrospect. Six years of instruction and relentless pressure from my father to practice, practice, practice had failed to produce a musician. I remember special performances at Stoatley Rough when visitors came, like Alice Salomon or other old friends and associates of our seniors from the German social welfare and women's movements. When Miss Fearon or Mrs Schwab came, English ladies on whom the financial security of the school heavily depended, I often had to put on a good suit and be one of the representatives of the student body for them to talk with.

Life at Stoatley Rough had its weird aspects. For example, we had virtually no money available to us, but our parents in Germany had lots. As a result, virtually every letter asked for things to be sent, odd things like a new watch band, ink for a fountain pen and even a new chain for my bicycle. and when the first chain did not fit, it was sent back to Germany for a replacement! Our parents in Germany functioned as our mail order house.

In July 1937, only about three months after arrival at Stoatley Rough, summer vacations came and I, like many of the other kids, went back to Germany to spend 5–6 weeks with my parents in Kassel. The mere fact that our parents considered it natural to take us home for vacations shows how relatively normal and safe they still felt their life was. Yet this was only a couple of months prior to the nasty affair with the female Department Head in what used to be our business described in Chapter 1, which drove them out of Kassel in a hurry. Once again I traveled in style, first class on the liner "New York" from Southampton to Hamburg, and on the "Europa", the fastest ship then, on my return. I remember the luxury of those journeys so clearly because they stood in such great contrast to the almost total lack of money, let alone luxury, we lived with in England. A Pound Sterling in those days was worth a lot, and to us it represented a huge sum seldom seen and rarely spent.

The Fall of 1937 was full of hard work, but also of the many pleasures Stoatley Rough offered. In addition to the music, there were plays, there was much intense human contact, student to student as well as with teachers; there were night walks, boys and girls, and many weekend hitchhiking trips exploring Southern England. The routine response to questions as to where we had been was "Beyond Liphook." It was said with a smile and became our shorthand for hitchhiking. Hitchhiking was not officially sanctioned, but it was silently tolerated by Astfalck/Nacken. There were no safety concerns in those days, other than perhaps the threat of a car accident, and many of the English people who stopped were intrigued by us and our stories and often very nice to us. We saw a lot that was interesting on those day trips—generally we could not afford to stay overnight—and cherished the adventuresomeness of it.

At the time, we often said to ourselves that if and when we would have our own cars, we would always stop for hitchhikers and swore that we would never pass them by. We tried to adhere to that undertaking at first, but as our cars filled up with children and life on the road became more dangerous, we did it less and less. Martha's Vineyard was an exception. We hitchhiked there ourselves, occasionally allowed the children to do so and we often still make pickups there, but only there. However, even now we feel a twinge of bad conscience whenever we pass a perfectly decent looking hitchhiker by on American roads.

Winter vacation 1937/8 was a big problem for the School. Many of the kids could not go home. Boys like me could go home but five weeks in Germany would not be good for our English. So Dr. Lion and others had to undertake enormous efforts making arrangements for us to spend time in English families. I was shipped to a very conservative family in Folkestone, on the Southern coast, for about a week. This is where I had my first real English breakfast, readied on the sideboard in the dining room by a maid, and everyone in the house could come in his own good time and help himself to scrambled eggs, bacon, sausage, cornflakes, etc. In Germany breakfast wasn't a meal. It generally consisted of a roll with butter and jam, and coffee for the grownups. I think it was also my first encounter with English tea sandwiches, those little triangles of soft white bread with a bit of cheese or cucumber in between. Other things were new. In Germany we were taught not ever to leave food on our plates; it was wasteful and impolite. Here, everybody left something. Scraping the plate clean seemed to imply that we hadn't got enough. Those unimportant differences in usage, of which there were many, contributed to our feeling—and being looked upon as—"foreign". The Folkestone stay included a big step forward in assimilation. Imagine: at night, the maid supplied a hot water bottle for my feet in my bed. After all, it was December and cold and wet, and there was no heating other than the fireplaces in every room. So everything felt damp: sheets, pajamas and the clothes you put on in the morning. It was an eye opener, in a way ununderstandable to me: here was an obviously well to do couple with a maid and two cars who lived with these, to us Germans, inconceivable inconveniences. But this was pre-war England, where central heating was considered "unhealthy" and cold houses, the pipes of which froze whenever the thermometer went below freezing, "good for you". My hosts went out of their way to be nice to me. They must have volunteered to take a refugee kid for part of his holidays. I wonder how strange and frustrating they found their guest. On my part, I found the stay interesting and enlightening, but I could not really warm up to these strange people. I do not think I was the type of good guest they had hoped for and, I think in retrospect, were entitled to.

My next experience that Christmas vacation was similarly strange to me and, I am afraid, unrewarding to my very kind hosts. I had the privilege of being invited for the Christmas/New Year's holidays to the Vernons, the people who owned Stoatley Rough, who lived in a beautiful townhouse in Hampstead. They were warm and kind to the foreign youngster with no home to go to for the holidays. But I, who had never heard of the magic of mistletoe, had never heard of stockings on the mantle or the type of thing one would find in them, had never seen a roasted turkey (only geese in Germany) nor had any understanding for what led grown people to wear funny paper hats at Christmas—of all times!—was utterly lost. It wasn't the Menorah I missed. I would have gladly settled for "Silent

Night, Holy Night", for serious singing around the tree, for serious presents, not jokes. I was so lost, I kept disappearing in my room. The fact that Baerbel was there too helped some, but she was much more at ease than I. How the well-meaning Vernons must have despaired of me!

Then came the final weeks of that complicated winter vacation of 1937/38. I spent them with my parents in Berlin. Having been driven out of Kassel, fearing for my father's life if they stayed, I found them in their nice apartment on the Jenaer Strasse in Berlin-Wilmerdorf. Their mood and that of all their friends was quite depressed and emigration possibilities were a major topic of conversation but, as already mentioned in Chapter I, there was still no real sense of urgency. My father remained to the very end too law abiding and too risk averse to do any of the "illegal" things some of his friends undertook. I believe that his inaction at this time weighed heavily on him for the remainder of his life.

On the whole, life was still too comfortable for people like my parents—and there were many—to act decisively on emigration. My parents could still, and did during this vacation, take me to Shakespeare plays in Berlin and to dinner in fancy restaurants. Nobody knew who we were. The time had not yet arrived when Jews had to wear the identifying Star of David on their clothes.

As mentioned previously, my sister Lisel had been at school on Monte San Vigilio in Italy since Easter 1935. But by the Fall of 1937 my sister wanted to leave. She had returned to Berlin before I got there on my winter vacation. At my parents' request, I had tried during the Fall to get Dr. Lion interested in offering her a scholarship. The Germans would not give permission to pay for a second child in England. Dr. Lion, who had also come to Berlin for that vacation, had a long interview with Lisel. That interview changed her original adverse reaction to a positive "Yes". Lisel consequently followed me to Stoatley Rough in February 1938. She, too, was assigned to the academic program. In fact, Dr. Lion clearly saw her capabilities and pushed her hard towards academic achievement. She took and passed Matric in 1939.

The Spring of 1938 is a blur in my mind of hard work for the forthcoming examination, much interaction with other boys and girls, and endless, long letters from and to my parents, worried about my future and theirs. I have recently found a folder of all my letters to my parents from 1937 to 1939. My mother kept them and considered them worth bringing along to America. They are fascinating as a reflection of the times, as well as my maturities and immaturities. Unfortunately, they are in German. Reading them recently has helped to refresh my memory in some ways and fix events in time. I began to urge emigration sooner rather than later; they saw all the obstacles and difficulties. South Africa, Argentina, Palestine and the U.S.A. were under primary consideration.

Sometime during that Spring the School allowed me to take my driver's license. I had to drive for some months with a red "L" tied to the front and rear bumpers of the School's small Austin, an open car with a rain roof and plastic side curtains when needed. Astfalck or Nacken, the only other drivers, had to be with me. Then I took my test in Guildford, including a U-turn on the steep High Street which I doubt would be tolerated today.

For some vacation round about this time I also went to North Wales under the auspices of some sort of back-to-nature organization. I remember Llandudno Castle, not much else.

Then came the successful Matric, except that it took from June to August 1938 to get the results. My close friend Baerbel left for America before we had our results. I sent her the congratulatory telegram to New York. We said a sad farewell. Her parents were already there, but their hard struggles in New York of which I had reported home were one of the many factors that slowed my parents' resolve to follow. Her father had been a much bigger man in the German Department Store field than mine, CEO of one of the two largest German Department Store chains, and yet he reported living a miserable existence struggling for a foothold in America.

Throughout the late spring and on into the summer and fall of 1938, my future hung in the balance. Should I go on with schooling? University was not even considered; too expensive and, in any case, "the Jews should have learned from their German experience that being in business or the professions just leads to disaster. What we need is more Jewish carpenters, electricians, plumbers and farmers"—so went the refrain from my parents and many other advisors. Dr. Lion, though generally of the same frame of mind, thought differently in my case, as well as my sister's. Accounting School somehow came up as a possible compromise. I spent much time in London and by mail investigating possibilities. I clearly did not want to become a plumber. In one letter to my parents I explained that though accounting school might be acceptable, I thought it was too confining and I would do better with the unlimited possibilities that I saw opening up from a general business course. On investigation, however, they were all too expensive for my frugal budget. Some sort of job during the day with evening classes seemed the best way out.

Dr. Lion to her credit—after all she was a headmistress not a vocational counselor—went to enormous trouble to help me find something. Ladies of the Jewish Council and other friends of the School were alerted and tried their best. I met with them, and even the son of Mrs. Schwab, the leading one of these ladies. The latter thought he could get me into the training program at Marks & Spencer. I had to write endless applications and present myself for interviews. There came wait after wait, and usually the possibility fizzled after weeks of hope. Thus the summer went by and the fateful Fall of 1938 dawned. I was still living at Stoatley Rough, making myself useful as a driver, a tutor and an Assistant Secretary to Dr. Lion. I had taught myself to type that summer. It wasn't a bad life. I was still quite happy at Stoatley Rough, I knew everybody well and all the ins and outs of the place and its people, but of course this life had no future for me, as my parents preached in letter after letter.

Little did they—or for that matter, I—know that, in fact then and there the most important part of my future was taking shape. Herta Lewent was Hilde Lion's secretary. She had come a few months after me and was about my age. She came as the School Secretary, and this was how Dr. Lion had her classified in her mind. Though at the same stage in life as those of us taking Matric, she was not allowed to participate in the academic program. It rightly upset her. We knew each other, of course, were friendly and had enjoyed playing tennis together, but in general our paths did not cross much until this post-Matric period when I had to find ways to make myself useful.

Herta's parents had managed to get themselves into England as well in the summer of 1938. They settled to a modest but safe life in London. Herta's younger brother, Helmut, came to Stoatley Rough, but at the much too tender age of 14 was assigned to the farm, to learn to become a farmer at the sacrifice of a broader and more rounded education. A grievous mistake.

Dr. Lion began to dictate to me, as well as Herta, and I took over when Herta had other things to do as School Secretary. Lion's form of dictation usually consisted of simply outlining the substance of what was to be said and then leaving it to us to write the actual text. It was good training. But I also functioned as a handyman. I drove her and Dr. Wolf and Dr. Lewen. I fixed broken lights and phone wires. Herta's office was tiny and it was no wonder that in those close quarters we got to know and appreciate each other very well.

At some time in the Fall or Winter of 1938, a rich Englishman, who had made a home and fortune in Argentina, got it in his head that he wanted to do something for refugee children. Through the Jewish Central Committee in London he was referred to Dr. Lion. His proposal: to take five to seven boys to Paris for a week. I was sent to interview with him. I did not particularly like him, but his proposition was irresistible: a week at the Hotel Vendôme, lots of sightseeing, all paid for by him. We went. I was the oldest and, so-to-speak, in charge, though our host and his male secretary really ran the show. After the frugality of Stoatley Rough, the Vendôme, our private suites and dining room, were an incredible experience for all of us. We saw a lot of Paris. I had never been there and it was an idyllic introduction. I talked to our host about my parents' plight and their vain efforts to get into Argentina. He not only promised to help, but assured me it would be easy for him to get anybody into that country. He called me back many times to talk about all he could and would do for us. I never felt comfortable with him but his very personal interest in my life gave me hope. After we returned I tried to follow up, but he cut himself off. None of the promised things ever happened. In retrospect and knowing more about life than I did then, it seems to me possible that he was gay and had some sort of hopes of enjoying us boys, but to the best of my knowledge nothing overt ever happened. It was a weird, but for us boys quite wonderful, experience. I am surprised that Dr. Lion, who should have known enough to be suspicious, took the risk.

Cultural travel was in the air then. I remember another trip with some other students to Stratford on Avon. We traveled on a shoestring, but somehow the money was found for us to go to the theater several times. How much organizing and begging that must have taken!

All this took place against the backdrop of a rapidly deteriorating political situation in Europe. Hitler's Germany knew no bounds to its expansionist ambitions. When Germany invaded Czechoslovakia, which Hitler had only a few months earlier undertaken not to do, England came to the brink of war, avoided at the last minute by Chamberlain's Munich Pact with Hitler, promising "peace in our time". It turned out to be but one year, an anything-but-peaceful one.

The coming War was in the air. Now, finally getting the Jews out of Germany took on the urgency it had lacked too long. My correspondence with my parents clearly reflects this change. But of course, with everyone suddenly feeling the same pressure, more and more doors closed. We had long been on the waiting list for a U.S. visa, but by now one could not even get into the U.S. Consulate to get an estimate as to how much longer the wait would be. It was a crucial question for those who saw some other, but less desirable possibilities. Should they take them or wait for America? Our correspondence is full of this sort of question. Argentina might be easier for older people, less pressure, less ruthlessness one thought; yet the U.S. offered more opportunity, particularly for the young people. Palestine, where my mother's brother, the early Zionist, was a dentist in Jerusalem, was another possibility. The fact that the U.S. did not open up its German quota, or make exceptions for truly threatened refugees—that Roosevelt did not even request it from an isolationist-dominated and partly antisemitic

Congress—is a shameful part of our history, as a result of which America cannot claim "clean hands" in the Holocaust tragedy. Though the unfathomable evil of the Holocaust was then unforeseeable, the very real threats to continued Jewish existence in Germany were by then obvious, and the threats to Jewish lives became clear after Kristallnacht in November 1938.

Meanwhile, Omi's, my grandmother's, continued life alone in Kassel with no possibility of visits from my mother had also become untenable. She, who was then over 70, was moved, first to Berlin and later—I do not know why—to Frankfurt. All those problems, too, were part of what I was expected to advise on by letter. Of course, everything was done by letter then. International calls were possible, but so complicated and expensive to make that they were reserved for emergencies. No e-mail or faxes. But: some things were a lot better then. Mail in England and Germany was delivered three times per weekday, even once on Sundays, letter boxes were emptied almost hourly, and one could rely on a letter between England and Germany getting to its destination the next day!

Which gets me back to Herta's little secretarial office. Herta, at Dr Lion's instigation but with very little supervision, had become engaged in a frantic, last-ditch effort to get Jewish children out of Germany. I helped her. We spent day after day together in her office writing letter after letter and receiving mostly frustrating but occasionally encouraging replies. Herta had, among other things, established a relationship by correspondence with a British vice-consul in Berlin who was prepared to stretch the rules and hastily issue visas to children so long as we could present some proof that they would not become a financial burden in England. This took much effort and imagination, the collaboration of many people, and endless volumes of correspondence necessitating many late afternoon drives to the Post Office in Haslemere. Gradually, Herta and I drew closer. There were night walks holding hands and, as time went on, she became the strongest magnet keeping me at Stoatley Rough. The political and professional uncertainties were there, but in a way they became a pretext; nurturing our relationship was the reality.

My first car accident occurred on one of those evening mail runs to the Post Office in Haslemere, pulling out of the parking space with inadequate caution. Could it be that my left arm around Herta Lewent's shoulder had something to do with that—quite minor—collision?

We continued to work frantically on emigration cases, and I tried to make myself useful in other ways. I remember spending many hours constructing a bell connection between Dr. Lion's bungalow and the main house. My feet were dangling from a trap door in the ceiling of Herta's office as I spliced wires, with her tickling my feet from below while I tried to "thread a needle" up above. Strange, the things one remembers! Anyway, we worked hard and we had fun.

My sister's best friend in Kassel, Liselotte Kaufmann, was still stuck in Kassel with her parents. Herta's efforts managed to get her on one of the "Children's Transports", mass evacuations of children without parents to England, and Dr. Lion accepted her as a household helper at Stoatley Rough. Her parents never made it out in time. She, too, eventually came to the U.S.

A cousin of my mother, who much later lived near us in Cambridge, Kurt Grunbaum, had been an active and militant Social Democrat in Germany. He was arrested by the Nazis under some pretext, but eventually was able to slip out of Germany to England with not a penny to his name. His sister, Rosemarie Heymann née Gruenbaum, lived in England by then in cramped quarters. Though Kurt's wife, Gertrude, and son were squeezed in, it was impossible to find a place for Kurt anywhere. Dr. Lion once again came to the rescue at our urging. She was instrumental in having a house on the Isle of Wight made available for just such refugees as Kurt, men without a roof over their heads, and she took the little son, Heinz, later Henry, in at Stoatley Rough for a few months. Her helpful tentacles reached far and wide. Even now as I am writing this we live only a few blocks from that self-same Henry Grunbaum.

Obviously, the influx at Stoatley Rough at this time was huge and we had long run out of space in the main house and the outbuildings created earlier. One of the large private houses on Farnham Lane became available and Dr. Lion decided to rent it. She let me do most of the negotiating of the lease of Thursley Copse, as the house was called, my first "legal" job. A young woman trained as an anthroposophical teacher, Thesi von Gierke, a relative of the previously mentioned, much revered Anna von Gierke, was put in charge of Thursley Copse, and I was moved down there as her assistant and jack-of-all-trades. The house filled with new kids almost over night. Who paid for all this, and for the teachers and food and clothes needed? Mostly the Jewish Refugee Committee, known as "Woburn House", but also to a large extent Nore Astfalck's genius at improvisation.

Then came Kristallnacht and the Nazi terror for the second time struck close to home. My mother was alone in Berlin; my father a prisoner in the Dachau concentration camp. My sister and I were advised of that by telegram from my mother. Now we exchanged letters several times a week. It was known that with connections and money it was possible to get these men, who had been part of the mass arrests right after Kristallnacht, released from concentration camp if, but only if, there was a guarantee that they could and would leave Germany promptly. Thus, all efforts had to be directed to obtaining a visa that guaranteed admission to another country—any country. My mother worked frantically to find a way out. She stood in endless lines at the American, Argentinean, South African and Palestinian consulates. She also tried hard for a visitor's visa to England. Her dream was to visit Lisel and me on the way to any ultimate destination. A permanent English visa was out of the question then. The British had been much more generous than the U.S. in the early Nazi years, but it appears that by this time they had decided to stay with the refugees they had, including those admitted temporarily as all of us students had been, but not to admit more.

These were anxious weeks for my sister and me and for many other kids at the School in the same situation. We were powerless. My letters are full of well meant advice to my mother to keep her spirits up and to be optimistic. Except for the English transit visa, where we had to supply substantiating letters, we could do little of substance to help. It was frightening and frustrating.

In late 1938, as I have described earlier, my mother managed to turn our long-ago charitable "investment" in an orange grove of the Hanotaya Fund into a preference visa for Palestine—at that time a British protectorate and, with that in hand, got my father out of Dachau and themselves out of Germany—alive, but, at 54 and 49 years of age, robbed of any sense of security or belonging and virtually penniless. Yet they were lucky. Many parents of Stoatley Rough kids did not get out. Auschwitz, Bergen-Belsen, Triblinka, Theresienstadt and the like were their then still unimaginable fate.

Through all of this I also had to stay in touch by letter and visits with all possibilities for a job for me or affordable training. One of the many threads I had been following resulted from my father having contacted an executive in the Gimbel Brothers department store organization in New York, a Mr. Arthur Kaufman, I believe, whom he remembered from some meeting of department store owners and executives years before. He must have asked for help for himself as well as for me. In early 1939, my following up on this lead resulted in my getting a job as a trainee in the London buying office of the Gimbel organization, smack in Oxford Circle. The pay was infinitesimal, but of course I learned something. We also looked on that job as a possible foot in the door for employment later in the United States. At that time Gimbel Brothers not only owned the second largest department stores in New York and Philadelphia, but also Saks Fifth Avenue and its sister store, Saks 34th Street.

So at long last I left Stoatley Rough, but only bodily and not in spirit. I returned almost every weekend to my "home". That meant a long tube ride to the farthest southern outskirts of London and then hitchhiking on the A-3, the main London-Portsmouth road. Hitchhiking having become a way of life for us at Stoatley Rough, my weekend hitchhiking trips from London to Haslemere came naturally.

Life with little money in one tiny rented room on Pond Street in Hampstead—cold, unless I had shillings to put in the gas fire—was difficult. In my memory, I haven't felt as cold again as in that London winter until the snowed-in foxholes of the Battle of the Bulge. But that was not the only source of discomfort. Stoatley Rough simply had not managed to make us feel at home in English surroundings. Even at that late date, I still felt very much the foreigner, and that feeling must have shown through, for English people also treated me very much as a foreigner and outsider.

Many years later I had lunch in Boston with Sir Hans Kornberg, the eminent English biologist, also a refugee. He told me that he, at age 11, after less than one year at Stoatley Rough, understood that he would never become "English" at this place and persuaded his guardian to transfer him to an English school. I had lacked that perception. More important, even if I had had it, I am sure I would not have acted on it, for nothing would have made me give up voluntarily the warmth, the feeling of comfort and home, that Stoatley Rough meant to me. As it turned out, I traded a lifelong German accent for a secure home at a crucial time in my development. I know now that I made the right choice, but that might not have been so if my life had taken a different course. All that matters here is to recall that those responsible for Stoatley Rough offered a valuable alternative for some of us refugee children—for better or for worse.

My job at Gimbel's served as a pretty good, though mild, introduction to business life. I had to get there by Tube on time, do the work that was assigned to me, keep a 45 minute lunch hour and do my part for the rest of the work day, which ended at five and with a terribly overcrowded Tube ride home—unless I chose to stay in town. I saw Stoatley Rough friends and occasionally went to the movies. There was little money for the better entertainments of London. My work consisted mainly of very routine tasks, checking bills against orders, assuring confirmation of shipments, etc. They did not tax my brain but nobody in that office taxed their brains. There were about seven or eight of us. The real job, the buying, was done by buyers coming in from the States. We were a follow-up office and provided a base of operations for them. It was interesting to meet the American buyers. They were hard-driving, brash fellows, very demanding, but also curiously polite to us "underlings". They seemed to be amused but not won over by the subservient attitudes of the English clerks. They insisted on kidding around with the latter, as if they were all on the same social level. Somehow that did not please my fellow Londoners; on the contrary, it made them quite uncomfortable. The differences were quite striking and interesting for me to watch and learn from.

But my heart was still at Stoatley Rough, and not just anywhere there, but very specifically with Herta. We had become very close. I often arrived at Haslemere late on Friday nights, would make my presence known by way of the window of the bedroom she shared with Inge Hamburger (later Pawlovsky), and then we would spend much of the rest of the evening and the weekend together. Our work on children's emigration continued on those weekends.

My parents did get their transit visa to England on their way to Palestine. I spent time with them in London and at Stoatley Rough. My father, remembered as the resilient traveler, motor cycle rider, skier and business executive, had changed. He was depressed and enormously worried about his and our future. Though he also talked bravely about attacking that future energetically, I could tell that his heart wasn't in it. My mother was so pleased to see us and to have all four of us together and out of danger, that she overcame the tribulations of emigration quite rapidly. They met Herta, of course, but nothing was said just then about our plans to make a life together. We were 18 and it seemed out of order to talk about it to them at that time. Planning ahead was just too difficult, though in our own minds we thought that we would somehow manage.

My father gave me a present on this occasion, a very large gold signet ring. He had it made in Germany by melting down a number of old German 20-Mark gold pieces which dated from pre-World War I and which had been given to me on the occasion of my Bar Mitzvah by one of my grandparents. The ring, worn by him as personal jewelry, had slipped by the inspections as they left Germany. That ring much, much later provided the gold for the two "HL" cameo rings which Herta and I have worn since the first year of our marriage. More about that later.

In the midst of all of this upheaval, arrangements also had to be made to get our good old Omi, my maternal grandmother, out of Germany. She managed to get herself to Jerusalem, to her son Ludwig, the dentist. She lived with him for the rest of her life. She died in Jerusalem in the late 1940s.

Our parents went on to Palestine. As previously mentioned, they suffered from the heat and their inability to find jobs. For more entrepreneurial undertakings there was no capital, though I also think that my father was simply not an entrepreneurial type. He had inherited a flourishing business from his father, the founder. He ran it successfully and grew it a lot, but he had never been challenged to create an economic enterprise from scratch, and he never did.

Meanwhile, war clouds gathered once again over Europe. The status of people like us, with German passports, in case of an English-German war was by no means assured. Once again worry and uncertainty about being alone in London if war should break out drew me ever more often and for longer periods to Haslemere, where life remained remarkably normal in midst of turmoil. Astfalck and Nacken in particular went out of their way to engage the worried students, many with parents still caught in Germany, and to help them overcome or live with their anxiety. They did so both by close and warm personal contacts and by making life at Stoatley Rough as challenging and involved, and as home-like as possible. Many of the kids owe their sanity to those two magnificent women. Yet these two women themselves had to deal with similar problems. They still had close relatives in Germany, would be totally cut off from them if war came and could not even be sure what England would do to them, non-Jewish Germans, in the event of war with Germany.

I was at Stoatley Rough when the declaration of War came as a response to Germany's invasion of Poland. It was a fearful as well as exciting moment, one of those moments in life one never forgets. I was with Herta in her office when one of the smaller kids whom we did not particularly like brought us the news through the window, with the grin of the messenger pleased to have been the first. We hated him for that smirk.

What frantic activity followed that news! Much of the School had to be transformed virtually over night. Before dark, all windows in that huge house had to be blacked out so that after dark no light could be seen from outside. No car could be used until its headlights had been fitted with a cover that allowed only a small slit of light to show through. The cellar and downstairs had to be made ready to receive all inhabitants in case of an air raid alarm, which was expected momentarily. Many of the children had to come to terms with the fact that their families were now behind enemy lines, totally cut off from them. (Perhaps fortunately, extermination camps were as yet unheard of.) The responsibility for all these children must have weighed heavily on those in charge. All this had to be dealt with against the uncertainty concerning the future status in England of this entire conglomerate of people with German, i.e. "enemy", passports in the most invasion threatened area south of London. And what if the Germans did come? Yet there was no panic. The frantic activity helped, as did the magnificent way in which all the grown ups and older pupils helped and supported each other and the younger ones.

The busy correspondence with my parents in Palestine continued throughout 1939. They were in touch with the U.S. Consulates in Berlin and Jerusalem, and

I was in touch with the one in London. We all knew this was the time to get out of Europe and its environs if one possibly could, and we could, for in late November 1939 our precious U.S. visas came through, covering all four of us.

The time had come to say goodbye to Stoatley Rough, to many friends destined to live through the War in England, and of course to Herta. We promised to write to each other, and did we ever—over 200 letters in four and one-half years! It was a difficult farewell, but there were many like it all around us. Permanent—or at least indefinite—goodbyes were the sad order of the day.

As is obvious by now, Stoatley Rough has meant a lot to me. Some of our best friends also date back to Stoatley Rough days, notwithstanding the many new friends we have made in the course of a busy and involved life since we came to America. Herta and I are still very close to Inge Pawlovsky, Herta's Stoatley Rough roommate. We still manage to see her regularly even though she lives near Paris. She and the Pachmayr twins, also Stoatley Rough friends, and I have skied together in Switzerland almost every year for over twenty years. And the old bonds never broke, like those to Inge Hamburger Pavlowsky in Versailles, Edith Hubacher Christoffl in Zurich, the Pachmeyr brothers in London and others who have since died, like Ernst Wohlgemuth, Lily Wohlgemuth and Peter Glueksmann, and Lilo Kaufmann Hutzler. We stayed in very close touch with Nore Astfalck, our children also got to know her. We taped an Oral History of her life during a week together in the Black Forest and have had it typed. She and Hannah Nacken returned to Germany after the War to help rebuild, and they were once again incredibly productive. Unfortunately, Hannah Nacken died early, a great blow to Nore. The latter worked effectively and energetically until days before she died. She was the star at age 89 of the first Stoatley Rough reunion which we helped organize in 1990. She died a few months later.

The reunion itself was the outgrowth of correspondence with my old teacher, Miss Dove, who became Margaret Faulkner after marriage. She, like Nore Astfalck, became a personal friend of both Herta and me and we stayed in close contact with her and her husband in Dundee, Scotland. Her life was greatly influenced by having taught at a refugee school. She became a committed volunteer in numerous organizations caring for refugees and prisoners of conscience all over the world. She died within days of our last visit to her in 1997.

As described at the end of Chapter I, Lisel and I traveled to New York on the "Statendam", a Dutch liner and by fortunate happenstance arrived in New York on the same day as our parents from Palestine. Like so many millions before us, we had not left Europe by free choice but entered America with great hopes for a new life.

3

NEW IN AMERICA

As mentioned at the end of Chapter 1, on one of the first days of January, 1940 our whole family of four, Mutti, Papi, Lisel and I, had been safely installed in a small furnished apartment on 40th Street in Long Island City just off Queens Boulevard. The reunion was joyful, but our parents' moods, particularly our father's, was somber, dominated by worry on how life would go on. We had $3000 to $4000 to our name, with the hope of getting some more money from sales of property in Palestine and by way of the prohibitively taxed money transfers still occasionally possible out of Germany, which was not yet at war with the U.S. Finding jobs was, therefore, the top priority.

As I recall our apartment, it was a bit like a railway train. You entered at one end smack into the living room. Then at the other side of the living room was a door leading into the kitchen, which included a dinette corner and beyond the kitchen was the bedroom. The living room could be, and was, converted nightly into a bedroom for my father and me. There was one convertible couch and one bed that came down from behind a door. Lisel and my mother shared the bedroom. The apartment's simplicity and small size did not bother us. We would not have been surprised if it had been a temporary shelter for refugees with dormitories and no privacy.

My sister's and my English was, of course, much better than our parents'. It was accented but fluent by then. Not so our parents. As time went on, our mother picked it up more quickly than our father. The difference between the generations in language knowledge caused a role reversal. Quite often, when contacts with the surrounding world were involved, we children had to be in charge and the parents had to act through us and with our help. It was the same in many other families of refugees whom we knew. I can see in retrospect that this must have been one of the many psychological downers of emigration for the older generation.

The next few weeks and months were spent by all four of us looking for jobs. My father still had some connections in the department store world. He made appointments to see loads of people whose names had been brought along from Germany and who had been contacted by mail from Palestine. All of those interviews were pleasant and encouraging and usually ended up with words such as "Let me see what I can do for you. You will hear from me." With German precision and lack of understanding of American politeness—often meaningless politeness—my father stayed close to the telephone on the days following such interviews confidently expecting to hear. Of course, he never did. He had not yet learned, as we all had to from experience, that those words really meant "Sorry, I wish I could help but I can't or won't."

Other contacts, of course, involved refugee friends and acquaintances who had been in the country longer than we. We went to see them all. Eventually, this led to a "stock boy" job for me in a small factory on 27th Street in Manhattan which, in a few rooms on an upper floor, stamped out sponge rubber toys shaped like ducks, frogs, dogs and the like. It was a marginal business run by a refugee and my job was to pack these products as they came out of the stamping machine into cartons, seal and address them, and then deliver them to retail distributors all over Manhattan. I was expected to walk when they were within 10 or 12 blocks, for example to the big department stores on Broadway and 34th Street, but was allowed to take buses or the subway when it was further away. I think a ride on buses or the subway cost 5 cents at the time, yet one had to count every penny. By this time summer was approaching, our first New York summer. My job scurrying around New York with packages turned into a sweaty, hot one. On the other hand, I gradually got my bearings around Manhattan and began to feel more at home. My salary, I believe, was something like $15 a week.

My sister's first job, at 17, was as a maid in Brooklyn, doing very menial work in the household of a professor. A short time later she switched to a small, refugee-owned lipstick "factory", a one-room, one-man and one-girl production line. Her salary was $13 per week. My mother also settled into a similar menial job through refugee connections. Hers was a primitive all-refugee-women assembly line producing simple beauty aids of various kinds. My mother, not so long before one of the grand dames of Kassel and the directress of one of the most profitable departments of our store, took to this job involving unskilled labor like a duck to water. She never showed the slightest resentment, did not get hung up with insults to her dignity and was delighted to make friends with the other women in the place and to make her first American money. She continued this positive attitude through the remainder of her life. This woman who in Kassel had liked to stay close to home and sleep in her own rather than a hotel bed, loved being in America, never looked back and, indeed, when much, much later it would have been possible for her to travel back to visit Germany, she refused. That was one place she never again wanted to set foot in.

My father had a much more difficult time. Yes, he did find jobs of sorts, but as I now know looking back, but we did not understand then, these were the hopeless, dead-end jobs in which no amount of effort was going to lead to any real success. Much of it involved selling door-to-door: Fuller Brushes, cosmetics, household brooms and cleaning materials and the like. Here was a 54 year old man accustomed to executive work, spending his days knocking without introduction on door after door in a city he did not know well enough even to judge the relative likelihood of success in a particular neighborhood. When the doors did open, his English was marginal which must have impeded his sales successes. Yes, he did make some money and was proud of bringing it home at night. But he was usually exhausted when he came home and nothing like the resilient and enterprising father I had remembered. Looking back on it, I can imagine the enormous willpower it must have taken to press yet another and another bell button, only to be insulted or sent away most of the time and occasionally selling an item for pennies of profit. It was a miserable life for him.

1940 was still the aftermath of the depression. Lots of Americans were out of work and faced similar poor employment choices. The only advantages which they had, and they were important, were that they spoke fluent English, they could exercise some judgement as to what jobs held promise and they understood the culture and knew what meant "Yes" and what meant "No" in the polite lingo of the day.

Eventually, our father graduated to selling textiles to wholesale houses. This involved traveling with a heavy suitcase on buses to the addresses of potential customers. It was hard, strenuous work but both financially and psychologically much better than door-to-door retail selling.

When we all had jobs, maybe four to six months after arrival, we moved from the furnished Long Island City apartment to a very much nicer apartment in Jackson Heights. It was in a big apartment, roomy, though still with only one bedroom and father and son sleeping in the living room. However, it was a great improvement over where we had been before, in a very much nicer neighborhood and we were able to furnish it ourselves, almost exclusively with second hand furniture. We were surprised and pleased at how much decent furniture could be acquired for very little money in America's antique and second-hand shops.

A little over a year after we had come to America, my sister received the offer of a full scholarship to Smith College. This fortuitous event came about through help from good old Stoatley Rough School. Hanna Nacken had a friend, Herbert Davis, who was president of Smith. Aware of Lisel's capabilities, she highly recommended Lisel to him for a scholarship at Smith. Once again I am struck by how ignorant of America we all still were at that time. None of us had ever heard of Smith College. We did not understand what a privileged opening to the American world a Smith degree would confer. We simply knew that it was a university equivalent and we understood the value of education. Thus, Lisel departed for Northampton in the fall of 1941. Her English Matric allowed her to enter as a Junior.

Lisel's departure for the first time since we had come to America allowed my parents to share a bedroom and me to have my own "bedroom", in actuality the apartment's doorless dining room.

I, too, realized that I needed more education. In the Fall of 1940, I enrolled in the evening sessions of City College, then "The College of the City of New York". It was not only free of any tuition charges, but was known to have a faculty that compared favorably with the very best. It had been, and still was at that time, a major breeding ground of American intellectuals who lacked the means to go to Ivy League colleges. The student body was heavily Jewish. There were hardly any non-Caucasian faces to be seen.

It was not easy to concentrate after a full day's work, but we all had to and did. There was no conventional college life—no sports, parties, drinking—but there was collegiality before and after classes and in the corridors. There was much highly charged political discussion. The vast majority of the students had quite extreme leftist views and Hitler's invasion of Russia had made communism respectable. Though my views were leftist, I was never won over by the Marxists and communists. I argued even then that, though a fine ideal, it was contrary to human nature and could never succeed. But there was also much stimulating discussion about what we were taught in our classes. I took an active part in it all and learned a lot.

Sometime in late 1940, I changed jobs. Having worked in London for the English buying office of Gimbel Brothers, I had met Gimbel executives and, through that connection, got a job, once again as a stock boy, but this time in one of Gimbel's affiliated stores, Sak's 34th Street. The Gimbel/Saks chain was so dominant and, indeed, a household world throughout America that it is still hard for me to understand that Gimbel's has totally disappeared from the face of the American business world. Only Saks 5th Avenue has survived.

My job was in the luggage and small leather goods departments. It involved restocking the main floor counters that sold wallets, key cases, cases for eyeglasses, etc. and the large luggage department on one of the upper floors. I also had to operate the machine in the luggage department which embossed initials on luggage, wallets and briefcases that had been purchased. It was a busy job but also turned out to be my first real window into the American world. For the first time all the people I was with all day were Americans. I learned about "kidding around", so important a facet of American life, about the necessity for surface friendliness with everybody, whether you liked them or not, and the value placed on hard work and the money it produced. I did work hard. Mr. Jack Mellon, the buyer and my top boss, got to appreciate and like me and gave me more and more responsibility. After about a year, when it happened that the assistant buyer quit, he offered me the job. My pay went from $15 a week to $25 a week, a lot of money then for people like us, and it established me on the first rung towards further promotions in the large Saks/Gimbel's hierarchy. I was pleased and considered myself successful. My parents were very proud, particularly my father who saw me following in his footsteps in the department store business.

Ever since we had arrived at Long Island City, and continuing in Jackson Heights, my father spent endless time corresponding with Palestine and Germany, trying to transfer funds from the Hanotaya organization in Palestine (the agricultural organization in which he owned an interest that had opened the door out of Germany and probably saved his life), and from Germany. The Jewish lawyer who had his power of attorney in Berlin, Dr. Sally Engelbert, made every conceivable effort to transfer our remaining German funds, subject to all the taxes and other confiscations disguised as legal withholdings that I have previously described. I still have much of that sad but then so very urgent correspondence. I was much involved, because by this time our parents did share all of the business problems with me and I could be helpful in interpreting both language and American circumstances. Eventually, these efforts succeeded in bringing some of the things left behind and some funds from Palestine and even some funds from Germany. My recollection is that when all was said and done, our total fortune in America amounted to between $12,000-$15,000. It meant that we no longer had to live totally from hand to mouth but it also was clear that if any of us stopped working, we would be destitute within a year or two.

What was my life like in those first two and one-half years in America? Really quite happy. I had a number of friends, refugee boys of my age who also lived in Jackson Heights or Forest Hills. We went to the beaches together on weekends, particularly after one of them acquired an old used car. There were girls around whom we befriended, all refugees, of course. There was no social contact outside of business with native-born Americans. We went to the movies, hung out on the street, worked hard and were quite satisfied with life. My parents, too, developed a social life with other refugees, some friends from Kassel and surrounding area and some newly acquired refugee friends. And we discovered American special-ties. My sister recalls that in her first $13-a-week job she treated herself to her first milkshake, and has been addicted to them ever since.

Most refugees in those years lived in Washington Heights in upper Manhat-tan. Those streets were full of men in overcoats that were too heavy and too long and had obviously been purchased in Germany years earlier. The women, too, wore the heavy German suits so unsuitable to overheated American apartments and had hairdos and wore shoes and blouses which instantly identified them as German refugees to passers-by. Jackson Heights and Forest Hills were the other refugee outposts, generally for people slightly better off. They mostly lived in apartment houses, very few had the means to acquire houses, and they too were easily identified by the clothes they wore and the way they walked and moved their hands as they talked. We younger ones quickly learned to emulate Ameri-cans and shed most of the old German clothes. We assimilated but still existed in an almost exclusively refugee environment.

Though life seemed reasonably stable to us then, the war in Europe raised black clouds in our minds and for our future. Hitler and his troops had success-fully overrun Belgium, Holland and France, and taking England seemed just a question of time. The momentum was on his side. Even in Russia he was making unbelievable progress and the fall of Moscow and Leningrad seemed imminent. This raised enormous worries about relatives and friends left in England and on the continent, and also raised questions about what would happen to us in Amer-ica when Hitler ruled all of Europe and North Africa. American Nazis were active, Father Coughlin could be heard daily on the radio sounding just like Hit-ler and we had little faith that with that devil Hitler controlling Europe, he would not find ways to take over America as well. Congress listened more to the Amer-ica First people, a strong lobby opposing American involvement in the war in Europe, than to those who saw the same danger we did. It is hard to imagine now just how very bleak things looked in 1941/42 for those of us whose very survival depended on the defeat of the Germans. Thus, although our daily lives went along fairly well, our long range outlook was grim and that affected everybody's moods.

In early December, 1941 my parents and I went to New Jersey to have dinner with the Walter Burchards. It was there, unforgettably, that we heard on the radio (there was no TV then) about Pearl Harbor and Roosevelt's "A day that shall live in infamy" speech. We were shocked and scared by the fact that now the Japanese at the other end of the world seemed to be as devilishly successful as Hitler in Europe and by the previously unimaginable destruction of almost the entire U.S. Pacific fleet in one day. On the other hand, we felt that the time had come for America to take sides—to take sides on the right side—and that, at least, encouraged us, though we remained enormously worried. We knew so little about America, but what we had seen seemed to make a major war effort hard to imagine if not impossible. How wrong we were!

I was 21 in 1941 and, as the new draft laws passed, my choices became clear. As a non-citizen, I could avoid being drafted but I could volunteer. If I volunteered, I would become a citizen immediately upon entering the armed forces. This was a war we strongly believed in and I had no question that I should volunteer. My parents naturally were ambivalent about this. They agreed that a commitment to the war effort was essential, but they hated to see me go and exposed to danger. In the spring of 1942 more and more young men disappeared from the places where we worked and enlistment was in the air. You began to be looked at strangely if you did nothing. I delayed action long enough to finish my second year of night school at CCNY. Then, in June or July 1942, I enlisted in the Army. There was a teary farewell from my parents. They once again had the hardest role. They were very alone.

4

IN THE U.S. ARMY

1. STATESIDE

Before I knew it, I was issued a uniform and all the other equipment necessary to make me look like a soldier and was on a hot, sweaty troop train to no one-knew-where. After days and nights traveling and waiting on sidings, we found ourselves in a place full of red clay and an almost unbearably hot sun, with no trees for shade. We learned that it was Ft. Bragg, North Carolina, the traditional home base of the U. S. Army's field artillery. We were lined up on the drill field by mostly southern sergeants who spoke a language I had trouble understanding and talked to by young, slim, good looking officers, also mostly southern, wearing the old broad-brimmed campaign hats of World War I—Smokey-the-Bear hats.

Then followed three of the physically toughest months I have ever spent, basic training. We got up early, started the day with calisthenics, then marched endlessly while sergeants bellowed at us for dropping one shoulder or not holding our heads straight enough or our chests far enough out, ran obstacle courses over and over and over again, with rifles and without rifles and had to learn to shoot those rifles at the rifle range. This was before the M1 rifle had made its debut. We had World War I Springfields which had to be cocked after every shot and had a tremendous kick to them. At chow call we stood in endless lines with our mess kits, got good—though as I now know, immensely unhealthy—food, ate it sitting on the ground and went on with our physical training. Every evening after an exhausting day we had 10 minutes to change into clean uniforms and then fall out and stand at attention while being inspected by the officers and watching the flag being lowered as a bugler blew Retreat. We were slapped on the fingers for dirty fingernails, kicked in the butt for not pulling it in far enough, made to stand at attention for 10 minutes if we moved our heads or even our eyes during inspection and lived through a good deal more of what was generally known as Army "chickenshit".

Dinner was in the Mess Hall, ample and, to my mind, very good, though the Americans complained endlessly about the food. It took me some time to realize that it was considered un-American not to complain about absolutely everything that the Army presented us with. "Bitching" was mandatory. We slept in barracks with upper and lower bunks. After the kinds of days we had spent, sleep came immediately and at reveille the next morning it seemed that we had only just retired. Bed making was another one of those routines we had to learn the Army way. It had to be absolutely perfect and identical to everyone else's. The slightest fold or deviation from the norm resulted in punishment, usually "KP", which meant kitchen duty. Of course, the cooks did the cooking. We KP's did the washing of the dishes and pans—pans big enough so that you had to climb into them to clean them—and endless filthy work disposing of garbage. It was the most hated job in basic training but no one escaped it for long.

Yet, gradually, in the course of those three months we did become soldiers. Our bodies grew lean and hard and forced marches for hours in the sun, which would have been impossible at first, now became routine. We marched at Retreat and at other formal occasions with perfect precision and began to feel proud of ourselves when throwing the rifle around to the commands of "Present Arms", "Shoulder Arms" and the like.

I was an average recruit. I did well enough not to fall behind, but I certainly was not one of the best. The obstacle course was a particular problem for me. I was never able to lift myself by my arms over obstacles and jumping from great heights meant overcoming all sorts of fears. I managed, and I managed not to stand out, which is probably the best thing you can do in the army, though in my case it was not due to forethought but rather to my not being physically the most agile and courageous nor the worst, by far.

Of course many of us realized that probably all this marching and drilling was not what the war we were training for would be all about. The fact is that in subsequent war action we hardly ever marched very far. We were mechanized and all long marches were on trucks. Nor was endless drill of much use in combat. Nevertheless, I think the Army knew better than we realized what it was doing. It made us physically fit, which was important, it made us learn instinctively and unquestioningly to obey orders, good or bad, sensible or foolish, and it instilled in us a certain pride in the outfit and camaraderie with our fellow soldiers, which are essential ingredients for success in combat.

I encountered no overt antisemitism or anti-foreign sentiment at this time, as far as I can remember. On the other hand, I was clearly not one of the gang. I still came across as a foreigner who spoke strangely, had trouble understanding Southerners and had no or inadequate knowledge of what every American knew and talked endlessly about, namely, baseball, football and basketball. Nor did I know at first, though I learned quickly, the Army's way of speaking, necessitating a cuss word in every sentence if possible, and in any event in every other sentence. However, the men around me seemed to accept me for what I was, an odd bird, but seldom made fun of me and they did help me as they would have helped anyone else when there was trouble at the obstacle course. We were ground into a unit of some considerable cohesion and pride in its accomplishments.

Of course there was much speculation as to what would happen to us as we neared the end of our basic training. When we first enlisted, all of us had to take batteries of tests, including an intelligence test. At this point, none of us knew our scores. However, at the end of basic training I was given orders instructing me to proceed by train to New York City. I did as ordered and, on the train, had an opportunity to read my personnel records, which were handed to me in a big yellow envelope. There I learned that, among other things, I had scored very high, my recollection of the score is 137, in the intelligence test. I mention this because that score haunted me for the next year, in that it destined me to go from school to elite outfit to school. I can see now that this high score also saved me from becoming a regular infantry soldier, the kind that did not survive for very long in the real war.

At a Replacement Depot in New York I was told to find my way to the Battery, locate an Army ferry to Governor's Island and report to First Army Headquarters. When I got there, I was assigned to the 518th MP Battalion. The last thing in the world that I had expected was that the Army would make me into a policeman, albeit a military policeman, but that is what had happened. Why?

It took some time to figure it out. It struck me soon after arrival that the quality of the men in this police battalion was head and shoulders above that of my basic training unit. Many of them were university graduates. All of them seemed smart. Probably my high IQ score got me into that company, though with barely two years of night school at City College I was one of the least educated in that group. First Army Headquarters, which later spearheaded the landing at Normandy and the drive through France, was at this time still commanded by an old, peacetime general, Hugh Drum. He was a spit and polish fellow and somehow had the pull within the old Army to form around him an elite battalion as his personal assistants and bodyguards.

1943

Pfc. Hans Loeser 1943

Now I was issued, in addition to very well cut khaki and olive drab uniforms, white gloves, white leggings, and white helmet liners. Next, I was taught to drive two and a half ton trucks as well as police-type Harley-Davidson motorcycles. When General Drum went into the city in his olive drab Chrysler limousine, two of us MPs rode escort in front and two in back with our motorcycle's police sirens screaming. Of course, we wore our white gloves, white helmets and white leggings. It didn't have much to do with the war, but it was enormous fun. Next, New York State decided to lower its speed limit to 40 miles an hour in order to conserve gasoline. General Drum had his bodyguard battalion deputized by the state police and put us out on the parkways around New York to help the state police enforce the new speed limit. Once again, it was a great lark for us young fellows. Repeatedly we stopped young women in beautiful convertibles heading out to Long Island estates and ended up playing tennis and having drinks with them at their homes. We did not take our duty with respect to speed limit enforcement very seriously and, if the truth be told, neither did our officers.

I did, however, learn how dangerous those motorcycles can be. We had lots of accidents. The worst accidents happened in Brooklyn and the Bronx where there were still lots of streetcar tracks. Once you get the tires of those big machines into one of those tracks, you were almost bound to crash. I managed to avoid those tracks, but quite a few of my comrades were not so lucky and ended up seriously hurt, a few of them died.

Another duty that befell us that winter was to ride shotgun on the crack trains then running between New York and Miami, the Champion and the Silver Meteor. Southern Florida had become the great training and staging area for what was then the Army Air Force. Every hotel in Florida had been requisitioned. Lots of military personnel traveled constantly from and to Florida on these trains. It was our duty to "police" them, i.e. maintain order, which in those early days of the War still included making sure that all of the buttons on their tunics remained buttoned and the ties pulled all the way up notwithstanding the temperature in those overheated railway cars. This is where I became an expert at dealing with drunks. Once again, we did our duty to the very minimum of what we could get by with. These trips introduced me to Florida in the winter. We left New York in ice cold weather, but by the time we got to Jacksonville it was warm and we opened the windows of the train and as we traveled south of Jacksonville the warm, moisture-laden air that envelops you in Florida first hit me. It was a very pleasant, new-to-me experience in mid-winter. Moreover, we got three days layover in Miami before we had to return to New York for another three days layover prior to the next trip. For several months we were pendulums going back and forth. The layovers in Miami were quite wonderful. We had nothing to do, swam in the ocean and had fun.

Sometime in the spring or early summer of 1943, the Army woke up to the fact that First Army Headquarters had to be transformed from a spit and polish peacetime outfit into a war time combat headquarters. Hugh Drum was retired and Omar Bradley took over. That was also the end of us geniuses in the MP battalion. We were quickly scattered all over creation. Many became front line soldiers. My orders, however, read to report to a certain headquarters in Philadelphia. There, to my amazement, I was told that I was to go to the University of Pennsylvania as a student, to be trained as an expert on Morocco, including learning to speak Moroccan Arabic. Why the Army would want to use a fluent German speaker to learn to speak Moroccan Arabic from scratch was beyond me, but I did as I was told. For the next nine months I was in what was then known as an ASTP program. We lived in the college dormitories and went to school from 8 in the morning until 6 at night. The language training continued until 8 at night. We were taught by linguistics Ph.D.s who initially knew no more Arabic than we did but managed to stay one lesson ahead of us. The real training came from Moroccans whom the Army had somehow whisked out of Morocco and brought to Penn. They were uneducated people who knew no English whatsoever. Their task was to speak the Arabic of the streets to our linguistics geniuses so that they in turn could create a phonetic alphabet to use to teach us the necessary vocabulary and grammar. We also had to talk with these Arabs from morning until night. It was a total immersion affair. We were not allowed to speak English except when addressed in English by a higher ranking non-com or officer. Lo and behold, we did learn Moroccan Arabic that way. After 4 months or so we could easily make ourselves understood and engage in simple conversations. We also learned a great deal about the culture, sociology and geography of Morocco and its inhabitants. This went on for 9 months. At the end, we were true Moroccan experts, understood virtually everything said to us in Moroccan Arabic and could easily converse in that language.

Alas, by the time we had reached that stage the Moroccan invasion had taken place and though there were still plenty of American Army units in Morocco, someone decided that we were no longer needed and those nine months were to be chalked up as wasted.

For me personally they were wasted. With no knowledge of the written language, I had nothing to hold on to and gradually lost all of the Arabic I ever knew. My knowledge of Morocco on the other hand stayed with me. Some others in our group made a career of this training. One of my buddies became a well known professor of Semitic languages at Queens College. Others, particularly those who knew Hebrew well, also found it easier than the rest of us to develop a greater understanding of Arabic and to use it in subsequent life.

By now I had spent something like 15 months since the end of basic training living a safe life as a private in the Army and learning things. But I was not contributing to a war effort in which I truly believed. Fearing that I would once again be assigned to yet another school because of my scores, I asked to be permitted to volunteer for the paratroopers. I signed all the necessary papers and waited.

There was another speculation that favored that course. Herta and I were exchanging letters almost weekly, and we had been doing so ever since I had arrived in America. We very badly wanted to meet again. We were aware that our experiences during the years of separation had been quite different and that we might find that we did not suit each other any longer once we met again. Our correspondence was still intimate and regular, but only person to person contacts could resolve whether we wanted to spend a lifetime together. Thus, I wanted to get to England as soon as possible, and I wanted to avoid at all cost being sent to the Pacific Theater of War, which was a very real risk. So I figured that the para-troopers would need me most urgently in Europe around the time of D-day, and this was another reason besides avoiding more Army schools for my volunteering.

When my orders finally came through to leave those comfortable dormitory rooms at Penn, I was instructed to report to a certain place in Washington, where I was put on a truck without being given a destination. We ended up in an Army camp in the Maryland mountains which was kept locked. There were no leaves and we were told that it was a top secret place. It was known as Camp Richie. It was an Army Military Intelligence training camp. So, once again, like it or not, I was in school rather than at Fort Benning, Georgia to become a paratrooper.

Camp Richie was a very odd place. In one way it reminded me of Stoatley Rough, because of all the German accents around. Even many of the officers spoke German-accented English. It turned out that some of the successful refu-gees, particularly people with names like Rothschild and Warburg, had obtained commissions in military intelligence and been posted to Camp Richie. Here we were taught endless information about the Order of Battle of the German army. We knew by heart which division was in what army and what army in what army group, what shoulder patches they wore and what types of people were thought to be in each. We were privy to all of the intelligence reports that came out of Western Europe and Russia about the German army at that time. We were also taught to read aerial photographs using stereo-optic readers, to identify German planes by their silhouettes and virtually everything else one knew at that time about the German land and air forces. We were also taught at great length how to interrogate German prisoners under front line conditions. We were trained for tactical interrogation, not strategic, high level questioning. It was highly interest-ing work where my German knowledge was, of course, very useful. I was by no means unique. Quite apart from the officers, whom I have already mentioned, virtually all of the GIs in my group either were refugees like me or were American university-trained German speakers.

By this time we were in the late spring of 1944 and the invasion of the Continent was rumored almost daily in the press. We assumed we would soon be shipped out to serve as intelligence corporals and sergeants in various combat units. Then, one day one of those lucky miracles happened which changed my life. Orders came down for a small number of us Richie students to be commissioned Second Lieutenants. I was among the chosen.

It is probably impossible for anyone who has not been in the service in the 1940s to understand the incredible change in one's life, self respect and duties which a commission conferred, particularly after almost two years as an enlisted man where I had never progressed beyond Private First Class. All of a sudden I no longer had to salute every passing officer, but I was saluted as I passed enlisted men, even sergeants and sergeant majors. The gratification of the first day of walking through the post and returning salutes rather than initiating them is hard to believe and probably not particularly admirable, but it was there. Though I didn't know it at the time, the fact that several years later I came out of the Army as an officer also made all the difference in the opportunities offered to me at the end of the war. Much more about that later.

Sadly, my father did not live to see me with gold bars on my shoulders and my cap, in officers' "pink" pants and dark green blouse, let alone live to see the defeat of Nazism, his nemesis. I had been home in New York on leave briefly after basic training and before reporting to Governor's Island and throughout my stay at Governor's Island I saw my parents almost every week. They were enormously proud of me in my uniform. If they were also fearful for my future, they never let on after the decision to enlist had been made. My mother had meanwhile changed jobs. Relying on training which she had received in the last years of World War I in Germany where, as described earlier in this story, she served in a well-baby clinic in Kassel, she hired herself out as a baby nurse. Usually she went to live in at the apartment of well-off Americans after a new baby was born and stayed with the new baby for six to eight weeks. Sometimes she did it on a day-to-day basis, sleeping at home. I think she got most of her jobs by way of mouth-to-mouth recommendation. She liked those jobs. She liked babies very much and it also opened a window for her into American life. Several of the families with whom she stayed became friends, and she continued to visit them in large part, I think, in order to follow "her" baby as he or she grew up. She was quite satisfied with her life. Working as a "servant" in other people's households did not adversely affect her ego one bit.

My father continued his struggle. He set off day after day with suitcases full of wares to be sold, sometimes at wholesale sometimes through retail establishments. Generally, I suspect, he was not treated well by his customers and his ego suffered enormously. This is so totally understandable to me now, though I must confess I did not think about it much in those days. If I had had to start afresh in my mid-fifties, say in Argentina, with no reserve funds in my background, limited knowledge of the language and none of customs and business affairs, I, too, would, I think, have suffered enormously psychologically and found it difficult to accommodate to such a situation.

However, by 1943 his struggles had brought some success. His work had impressed one of his employers and he was put on a salary, perhaps plus some commission. But in the fall of 1943, traveling on the open top of a 5th Avenue bus with heavy suitcases in mid-summer heat, my father caught a debilitating illness. He came home and went to bed. First it was thought to be "the grippe", later a severe case of pneumonia. When he failed to improve, the doctor told us that there was a new family of drugs, the sulfa drugs, which were available only to the armed forces. He thought that it would take a strong dose of sulfa to cure my father. I then made an effort to obtain sulfa from our army dispensary, first explicitly and then later through subterfuges, but nothing worked. His condition worsened and ultimately his heart was affected, I believe, and he was taken to the hospital. He did not improve and after several weeks of illness died in the hospital on September 13, 1943. He would have celebrated his 57th birthday later that month, on September 30th.

I was luckily able to visit him often and, upon his death, to get a few days of compassionate leave. It was a tough blow to all of us, though in retrospect I believe that my father had lost the will to live and that this contributed to his inability to recover from his pneumonia. It was a terrible blow to our mother after twenty-four years of marriage.

I remember that I had the sad duty of attending to the funeral. Once again, we were totally ignorant of American customs in this regard. The hospital referred us to a funeral home, and I made all the arrangements with that organization. They were pleasant enough, but utterly and totally impersonal. We had no memorial service of any kind. The body was cremated and a day later I traveled with an employee of the funeral home in that employee's car to a Jewish cemetery somewhere up the Hudson River, I think in Westchester County, with a little tin with my father's ashes on the back seat. At the cemetery, a grave had been prepared, I put the can of ashes in that grave, someone handed me a prayer book and I said Kaddish as best I could, threw some earth on the grave and then went back with this stranger to New York City and my outfit on Governor's Island. It was a trip I never forgot but, unfortunately, I never took in the name or location of the cemetery. My thoughts were elsewhere. I do not know to this day where he is buried.

Though my father was saved from extinction in a place such as Auschwitz, he was clearly a victim of the Nazis. In the first place, his six weeks in the concentration camp Dachau did impair his health, robbed him of a great deal of energy and resilience, and speeded up the loss of self-confidence and belief in the future which had begun with the sale of his business. The year in Tel Aviv, where he also scurried around unsuccessfully looking for ways to make money or start a new business, did not help. There were too many others like him engaged in the same desperate effort. And then came the frustrating years in New York which gave him little hope for a silver lining in his very gray sky. The fact that some others of his friends, also refugees, were succeeding in building up new businesses did not help, I am sure. Though money can never compensate for a life, the only positive thing that much later came out of these sad events was that the German government had to pay substantial amounts in compensation to my mother, which made her financially independent for the rest of her life. More about that later.

Lisel after reading the above gave me a new insight. She recalls having been told by our mother that, when they were first married, my father really wanted to be a medical doctor and did not want to be saddled with taking over his father's business. However, as was customary in those days, the parents' wishes in such matters prevailed. He gave in to family pressures and became a business executive, rather than a doctor. If that is true, it explains a lot about him to me.

Indeed, I firmly believe that I, too, was not cut out to be an entrepreneur. Luckily, as described later, through a very haphazard process at the end of the War, I became a lawyer and did not return to the retail business I had been in before entering the Army. I am a very good lawyer but feel sure I would not have gone nearly as far as a business executive as I have in the law. Even as primarily a business lawyer, I excel at analyzing well, exercising judgment, and being an advisor to the decision makers. Entrepreneurship, which takes different qualities, I like to leave to my clients. My father may have had similar abilities and limitations, but was forced in another direction with his heart not in it. I feel enormously sorry for him as I write this.

It is interesting to speculate whether I might have been faced with the same pressures had it not been for Hitler. The Nazis certainly managed to make my life much more interesting and rewarding than I suspect it would have been had I followed in my father's footsteps. It is the older generation, that of my parents, that suffered most cruelly.

Meanwhile, my sister had graduated from Smith with a BA in philosophy and that same fall of 1943 had gone on to Bryn Mawr College, from where she graduated with an MA in history in 1944. To jump ahead a bit, she then took a war job, but an interesting one, as a researcher in the African Department of the Office of Strategic Services in Washington. She stayed with the Research & Analysis Division of OSS as it became part of the State Department after the War and later when it became a unit of the newly created CIA. It must have been around late 1946 or in 1947 when my mother finally decided to give up the Jackson Heights apartment and to join Lisel in a very nice garden apartment in Silver Springs, MD.

2. BACK TO ENGLAND

It must have been late May, 1944 when the new-baked 2nd Lt. at Camp Richie received his orders to proceed by troop ship from New York to "somewhere in England", but our ship did not leave until several days after D-Day, June 7, 1944. It was a lengthy passage taking a zig zag course across the Atlantic escorted by destroyers all around us and air cover as we approached Ireland. It was a huge convoy of 50 or more ships carrying a precious cargo of thousands of soldiers and supplies to England at a crucial moment in the War. At that time, no one could be sure that the small beachhead that had been won in France at enormous cost in lives could hold against counterattacks.

On that troop ship I learned once again what a difference it made in those days to be an officer. In the holds of the ship the enlisted men slept 4 bunks deep in incredibly crowded and poorly ventilated space, with only the poop deck to come to for fresh air. We officers had staterooms, two to a room, and the run of the rest of the ship, including deck chairs on the boat deck. That differential extended to the elegant mess hall in which we were fed as opposed to the long lines with mess kits in hand that the enlisted men had to go through to eat Army chow. As Irving Berlin's song goes, "This is the Army", and those long-standing customs differentiating between a "gentlemen class" of officer and everybody else were generally accepted. How lucky I considered myself!!! But for the fortuitous commission handed to me only a few weeks earlier, I, too, would have been in one of those holds below.

We landed in England without mishap and boarded a train without being told where we were headed. It was an endless journey. I think we spent two nights just sitting on sidings while trains with higher priority were allowed to pass. The thirst of Omaha and Utah beaches in Normandy for more men and supplies came first. After a bus ride, we finally found ourselves in a picturesque, small English town, which turned out to be the lovely town of Broadway in the Cotswolds. All of us officers were billeted in English private houses, mostly with families or, in some cases, in houses that had been emptied of their inhabitants and requisitioned. I was in one of the latter. Gradually it appeared that Broadway was a center where specialized officer replacements were collected, to be dispatched where most needed in France.

As soon as I could figure out a way, I left Broadway for a neighboring town. One of the other advantages of being an officer, I learned, was that I could go to the local Army motor pool and ask for a Jeep, which would be signed out to me on request. From the next town, I made my first telephone call to Herta in London. It was total surprise, for Army censorship had not allowed me to tell her that I was on my way. Though I was not allowed to tell her on the phone that I was in Broadway, I did manage to describe where we were indirectly and we arranged a first meeting after four and a half years that following weekend.

That weekend we met. It was momentous and, at first, awkward. Our love affair had been sustained by many hundreds of letters, but we both knew that now came the real test. We were both almost five years older than when we had last seen each other, had had lots of experiences, different experiences, had lived in different countries, and had both had relationships with other boyfriends and girlfriends, respectively. There was a great deal of sniffing each other out and talking endlessly. But by the end of that first encounter, I think we had both pretty much resolved that our lives belonged together. Of course, the war overshadowed all of this. I could be sent off to France any day.

Herta 1944

My recollection is that she came back once more for a visit during which we became very much closer and that there was one more visit with her father after she had told him we wanted to get married. On that visit I rather formally asked him for his daughter's hand and received his approval—enthusiastic approval, I believe.

Like most wartime couples, we planned to get married before war action would suck me further in, with an unknown outcome. However, we didn't get a chance to do that. I applied through channels for permission to get married, as one was required to do. The response that came back "By command of General Eisenhower" was that permission was granted, subject however to a 90-day cooling off period. This was ironic. That sort of order, which was routine at the time, made a good deal of sense when GIs who had met an English girl the night before asked permission to marry her the next day. For us who had known each other for more than six years and had written letters to each other for four and a half years, it was ridiculous. But "This is the Army ..."

Shortly after this, Army action did claim me. To my surprise, the Army somehow remembered that I had once volunteered for the paratroopers and, therefore, assigned me to the 82nd Airborne Division which had spearheaded the Normandy landings, dropping behind the intended landing beaches during the night before D-Day. The Division had suffered enormous casualties both during the landing and in the several weeks of crucial fighting afterwards until the beachheads were secured. The two airborne divisions involved, the 82nd and the 101st, were then withdrawn back to England to be readied for the next airborne drop. I, with thousands of others, were replacements for the men lost in Normandy.

I reported for duty to 82nd Airborne Division Headquarters at a then secret location near Leicester. There I was informed that I would be the officer in charge of an intelligence detachment of two officers and four enlisted men, two jeeps and a trailer full of intelligence equipment, attached to regimental headquarters of the 325th Glider Infantry Regiment. The 325th was the only glider regiment in the 82nd. The other two regiments—sometimes three for particular operations—consisted of parachute regiments, the 504th, the 505th and the 508th Parachute Infantry Regiments. For one reason or another, the other officer never showed up so that it was myself and four enlisted men. I met them all after I reported to regimental headquarters. We were all German refugees speaking English with distinct accents. Our principal function was interpreting German material such as letters, books, orders captured in action and the front line interrogation of prisoners of war. We generally operated just behind the front lines, working with company or battalion headquarters personnel, though in the chain of command we were attached to regimental headquarters.

One of the sergeants on my IPW team in
front of our glider in England 1944

The 82nd by that time was a seasoned combat outfit which had seen the heaviest action. These were real veterans of recent combat and they were still full of what they had been through. We heard much talk about what it was like to try to get out of a glider that had crashed in the hedgerows of Normandy under German fire and about buddies that were killed or horribly maimed. On the other hand, these were also troops that were enormously proud of what they had accomplished. The esprit de corps of that outfit was incredible and infectious. Combat survivors often think that nothing can happen to them, that they are supermen destined to be lucky and that, notwithstanding all the death around them, they could accomplish almost anything without being hurt. It was a superman's spirit carefully fostered by our leaders and, of course, that sort of spirit is what makes elite combat troops accomplish the feats they do. Small things that distinguish you from other soldiers, such as the high jump boots laced in a particularly fancy way and the glider or parachute wings worn on your chests and caps make all the difference to the morale of such an outfit.

We newcomers felt strange among those seasoned veterans, but were treated well and respected for the use they thought they could get out of us in the next operation.

We were totally cut off from communication with the outside world. We were allowed to write letters from "somewhere in England" but were not allowed to write about where we were or what we were doing, and could not otherwise communicate with people in England. We were receiving replacements at an enormous rate and there was a lot of maneuvering and drilling. Those of us who were new to the glider infantry learned what that was all about and went up on numerous training missions. Our gliders had a tubular steel frame covered with canvas. There was room for a jeep or a small "airborne" 75mm. howitzer, or a squad of 12 men in the body of the vehicle plus a pilot and copilot up front. The cockpit was hinged at the top and had latches at the bottom. There was a wire that ran over pulleys in the ceiling to the back of any vehicle in the body. The intent was that, after the glider landed, the vehicle would start its engine, one person would unlatch the cockpit section and then as the vehicle started driving the cockpit would rise on its hinges and the vehicle would drive out. It was a wonderful theory for a quick escape from an aircraft that was bound to be a target immediately after landing. In maneuvers, it often worked. In actual combat, it almost never worked for the simple reason that a plane that had crash landed, and almost all did, had its fuselage thrown out of line and no amount of tugging on the wire was usually able to raise the cockpit. This meant an endless struggle to raise it by hand or chop it to bits in order to get the men and the vehicle out of it. The whole purpose of gliders in an airborne landing was to bring in heavier equipment than could be dropped by parachute, such as jeeps and howitzers, or to bring in whole squads of men which would be concentrated in one spot, rather than the scattered paratroopers whose landings were likely to cover a large area. Our task was to try to form a core until the paratroopers could gather.

Since our small unit was expected to function in combat just behind the front lines at company and battalion levels, I made sure that my men with their German accents would be well known by the people with whom they would serve in combat. Our functions were coordinated, in turn, by a similar refugee-dominated team of intelligence officers and sergeants at division headquarters and so on up the chain of command. Every few days we got updates based on the latest intelligence from the Continent about the German armed forces facing the advancing Allies, their strength, their losses, their commanders, their home areas, their insignia, and the like, all information that might be helpful in interpreting documents and interrogating prisoners. There were people at higher headquarters who had learned to impersonate prisoners, and we had endless trial runs as interrogators with them, sometimes lowly privates, sometimes lieutenants, captains or colonels. It was interesting work. We were, of course, strictly forbidden from using physical torture to make people talk, and never did. Under the Geneva Convention, prisoners of war need give only name, rank and serial number. Ours was the job to break through that code without violating the Convention. Camp Ritchie had trained us to do so, and we were very often successful, using mostly psychology, shows of superior knowledge, kindness, unkindness,, and other means of non-physical seduction and stealth. In general, it was expected that we would focus on tactical interrogation, such as identifying units, locating artillery emplacements and machine gun nests in the immediate vicinity and trying to get the plans of the enemy for the next day or two. While more strategically valuable material might fall into our hands and we were therefore trained to recognize it, we were expected to send that on expeditiously to higher headquarters for interpretation.

In late August and the first two weeks of September 1944 we were ordered two or three times to airfields for combat missions. We were in tents on the fringes of the airports, there were long lineups of troop carrier planes and gliders and we waited. We were issued rations, ammunition and all the rest and then sat, and sat, and sat. Several times we actually boarded planes ready for takeoff, but each time the operation was canceled and we went back out. This was a nerve wracking time. In the end, when the real thing came, none of us any longer believed that it would be anything other than a trial run. It was not foolishness that brought about these false tries. We were always supposed to land ahead of the advancing troops, to take and preserve bridges or other strategically important targets. However, First and Third Armies moved so unexpectedly fast in those weeks that they usually got to those targets without our help.

Our airplanes were all C-47s (DC-3s), twin engined Douglas transports. They each carried about 20 paratroopers or towed one, or in combat sometimes two, gliders. The gliders were attached by a long elastic tow line from the tail of the tow plane to the nose of the glider. We had a lever in the glider to cut loose at our option. The glider in combat had only one pilot, on maneuvers a pilot and a copilot. These were generally Army Air Force warrant officers. There was a telephone line in the tow line so that the pilots could communicate with the tow ship pilots.

In the air in our glider 1944

What I learned quickly on maneuvers is that though gliders look as though they "glide" silently through the skies, this is not true for Army gliders. In the first place, they make a lot of noise because the prop wash of the tow plane makes the canvas slap against the tubular frame. In the second place, they tend to whip up and down and sideways in that prop wash. It is a very unpleasant ride and more than half of the occupants of the glider usually get airsick. The bottom of the glider tended to be a smelly mess.

3. COMBAT IN EUROPE

On September 16th, we officers were assembled in one place and told by our Division Commander, General Gavin, that if things go according to plan, the Division would take off in several echelons early on the 17th on an operation code-named "Market-Garden", involving an airborne landing just outside the German-held Dutch city of Nymegen. We would be part of a three pronged mission of XVIII Airborne Corps, intended to take the bridges across the lower Rhine before the Germans could destroy them. We were then to hold those bridges until the British Second Army attacking north from Belgium would reach us, cross the bridges and then be free to outflank the heavily fortified German lines west of the Rhine, the "Siegfried Line." The 2nd Army with us and other U.S. units attached was then to race towards Berlin across the North German plains which were unfortified. The 101st Airborne, our sister division, was to take several smaller bridges near Einthoven, we were supposed to take the very large and important bridge across a branch of the lower Rhine at Nymegen, and the 1st British Airborne Division, reinforced by a Polish airborne brigade, would take the northernmost bridge at Arnhem. As a result of the devastating Normandy experience with gliders in the lead, our glider regiment would not go in with the first echelon but probably with the second or third, later on the 17th or the next day. And that's how it turned out.

We watched hundreds of planes full of paratroopers rise into the sky from our airfield and from several other airfields nearby and then circle overhead to form into a formation that covered the sky as far as the eye could see and then head to the Continent. It was thrilling to watch. Herta told me later that she, like so many others in southern England that Sunday morning, saw it too, but it made her full of fear. I had written that I might be "out of touch" for a long time soon, and that awesome air armada filled in the rest for her. Luckily she was with Hannah Nacken at the time who was enormously supportive

We had no news as to what happened to them, though we boarded our planes and gliders repeatedly without taking off. I don't recall if we went in on the afternoon of the 17th or later. Anyway, the on again, off again routine dulled our senses so that when we finally did take off, few of us knew what day and what time it was. Once again we formed in the sky into an absolutely enormous formation for this second wave. There were planes with parachutists and planes towing gliders as far as the eye could see all flying low at assigned altitudes. As we headed towards the Continent hundreds of fighter planes came from all over England to fly cover above us and our fighter bombers paved the way below us. It was an unbelievably spectacular event. I know that many people in England, who saw it from the ground, will never forget the sight. It was most impressive for us too, in midst of it.

Until almost the end, our air journey was rather uneventful except that all of us were airsick. For purposes of this mission I had a jeep and four men in the glider and I was riding in the copilot's seat. Had anything happened to our pilot, I do not think I would have been competent to bring the plane down. I had had some rudimentary training but had never actually handled the controls. Shortly after we passed the coast, we began to encounter fire from flak batteries. One didn't hear them and seldom saw the flash of the gun muzzles. What we did see was the puffs of smoke in the air where the shells exploded. Occasionally, we saw a plane or a glider get hit and go down, but mostly the formation held. As we got closer to our landing zone, the planes went to an even lower and more exposed altitude. 1500 feet was the optimum height for cutting loose. The navigator up front was supposed to tell us when to cut loose. Very shortly before we got to our drop zone, my tow plane's right wing was cut off by what looked like machine gun fire from the ground. There were certainly no German fighters in sight. We saw it happen and our pilot cut us loose, putting us in a steep dive down while the formation went on very briefly and then cut loose its gliders and dropped its paratroopers. We could see this in the distance as our glider lost altitude as rapidly as possible. A slow, landing glider is a sitting target. Our pilot headed for what seemed like a lonely farmhouse, tried to land in its garden, but would have hit the house if, in the last minute, he hadn't been able to lift the plane just over the roof of the house with its last bit of lift and then plunked it down in front of the house. As usual, it was impossible to open the front of the glider as we had been instructed to do but, after a struggle taking 10 or 15 minutes, we did open it far enough for the jeep to get out. Luckily, we were not under fire; we heard a lot of combat going on in the distance, but all was quiet where we were. The farmer and his wife were flabbergasted to see us there but once they collected their wits were enormously helpful. With his help and his wife's we managed to tow the glider, the canvas of which was in shreds, into a barn tail first, with the wings sticking out. We then packed down a lot of bushes and trees to cover the wings as much as possible so that they would not be easily discerned from the air. Then we hid in that house for the rest of the day until dark and after dark the farmer carefully instructed us how to follow various side roads to what we showed him on the map was our drop zone. Without lights and at a walking pace we drove that route, by that time mostly worried about being mistaken by our own perimeter people as Germans. Luckily, our glider pilot spoke flawless southern-accented

English. The rest of us kept our mouths shut. Eventually we got challenged in English and responded properly, and were welcomed by an advance squad of the 504th Parachute Infantry. They directed us towards the center of the perimeter which had been formed and we found our regiment, with our jeep and men intact. Jeeps at this point were at a premium and highly valued.

By this time almost all German soldiers had been cleared from most of Nymegen. The paratroopers held a perimeter around the town but there was heavy fighting near the bridge approaches. We settled in a Dutch house the occupants of which must have either fled or been kicked out and very soon German prisoners began to show up for interrogation. We finally had a chance to do what we were trained to do and, I think, did it well.

It took until the 19th or 20th for the British 2nd Army vanguard, the Guards Armored Division, to reach Nymegen, much longer than planned. This was the signal for the 82nd to take the great bridge, with armored support. Our troops made a daring daylight crossing in assault boats under heavy fire and took the far side of the bridge before the Germans could blow it up. We and they took enormous losses. Of course, as is usual in war, I had only the most sketchy information at the time of what was going on. We had our job to do and except by rumor knew little of the bigger picture. I believe that the information which we gathered from prisoners was quite useful in identifying the strength of the units on the German side of the Vaal River, which is the name of this particular branch of the Rhine estuary.

Operation Market-Garden has been amply written about and pictured in the film "A Bridge Too Far" so that I don't need to go into details. I do remember the bitterness of our officers and men who thought that their bravery and losses of many friends had been wasted because the Guards Armored settled down to drink tea, as we saw it, rather than drive on towards Arnhem. As is generally known, the British and Polish Airborne troops at Arnhem ran unexpectedly into very heavy defenses by two German Panzer divisions which had recently moved there to rest and whose presence was not known to our intelligence. The British Division held as long as it could, waiting to see the lead tanks of the Guards Armored Division at any moment. They never came, the British and Polish airborne were essentially wiped out and the crucial Arnhem bridge was never taken.

An all out effort to break through to Arnhem would have been difficult, because all the roads in this area run on top of dikes, where tanks are sitting ducks, but this had been known all along and the Second Army had such enormous strength in armor that we, amateur strategists, all thought they ought to go rather than stop. Their leaders decided not to risk it. As a result, the grand plan of

Operation Market-Garden failed. A good chance to end the war quickly was lost, at the cost of the ferocious fighting and huge losses of the winter of 1943/44. There was enormous bitterness about this in the two American divisions. We blamed Field Marshall Montgomery's lack of decisiveness for pulling a defeat out of what we saw as an almost certain victory in sight. We regretted our heavy losses in taking "our" bridges in vain, but we also felt great solidarity with the airborne troops in Arnhem, who had been left in the lurch.

We spent the following two months in and around Nymegen holding a stationary position with lots of patrol activity. Our troops hated it. They had been trained to take ground, and then get out. Trench warfare was not their thing. We got prisoners to interrogate almost every day and a good deal of other material of importance, which we either interpreted or forwarded or both. We rendered useful services, but at this point were quite comfortably established in the town of Nymegen, had good food and were not exposed to daily danger, though occasionally a long range German shell would land in Nymegen. The Dutch people were wonderful to us. We were invited to their homes, though they had nothing to eat and our rations when given to them constituted Ritz-like food to them, who had starved for years. We even had a house set up for hot showers, through which various units rotated on a schedule. It was not a bad life though the front line was less than a mile away.

Eventually, probably in mid-November our Division was relieved at the Front and we traveled by jeep and truck to what had become our rear base near Reims in France. Life here was easy, the champagne flowed freely. Officers were given a free ration of two bottles of liquor of their choice per month and could buy more at the PX or from the French people. The great champagne cellars of Reims had been raided by the troops who first took Reims. I visited one of those cellars. It was a mess. You waded in champagne. The soldiers had often broken the necks off bottles, drunk a little and tossed it away. Much went on that, in retrospect, one couldn't be particularly proud of. French girls were hungry and lonely and Americans were big and well fed and had food and nylons to give away. The synergies were clear.

We were enjoying one of the good sides of being in a crack airborne division. Dozens of other American divisions, like the 1st and the 9th which went into Normandy in the first wave, had to go on and on with replacement after replacement and long periods of relief were unheard of. A few days in a rest period just behind the lines was the best they could hope for. We, the airborne, were too valuable for that. We were thrown into the roughest combat, but then were generally pulled back again into a place like Reims, far from the front and designated as "Theater

Reserve", which meant that we were the ultimate reserve of the Theater Commander, to be thrown in for special operations or emergencies.

Hans and his airborne jeep 1944

Meanwhile, the story of General Eisenhower imposing a 90-day waiting period on me, delaying my getting married to a girl I had known for many years, had caused a great deal of mirth in the officers' mess. It represented the sort of routine unthinking application of rules to a situation not meant to be covered for which the Army was notorious and therefore was great food for the normal bitching routine. It made me better known in the Division than I might otherwise have been and, in the end, had quite a wonderful result.

One day in December I was told that I was to report to the Chief of Staff of the Division. He said "Lieutenant, do you still want to get married?". I said "Yes sir". "Is the 90-day waiting period up?" I said "Yes Sir." "All right. There is a troop carrier command pilot who also wants to get married and his waiting period is up. I will issue orders for both of you to proceed to England on temporary duty and will authorize the use of a troop carrier plane for this purpose. Your duty will be to get married as promptly as possible, have a few days with your bride and then get your asses and the airplane back here to us. Take off!" I said "Yes Sir. Thank you Sir." and left in a hurry.

And that is what happened. The two of us flew our "private" DC-3 to an Army Air Corps field close to London, took Army transportation into London, and then I started to chase Herta down. It took a great deal of patience amidst my understandable impatience. She had a secretarial job in the Knightsbridge area and her parents whom I called thought that, if she was not at work she might be with Sonja, a girl she worked with and was friendly with. I did not find her at her job. All I could do was leave messages and I finally settled down to a longer-than-I-liked wait outside Sonja's flat. We finally connected and fell into each other's arms as she unsuspectingly returned with Sonja from a fair they had attended. What surprise and what joy! It must have been December 9th that I arrived. On December 11th we had a civil wedding at the appropriate Registry Office, and then had a party given for us by the Kochmanns, close friends of the Lewents. Inge Hamburger was present also, as was Herta's brother, Helmut. Then Herta and I boarded a train to Torquay on the south shore of England, the warmest place we could think of in England in December, where we found, or perhaps had rented in advance, a small room with a bath in a rooming house. The double bed took virtually the entire room. When you left the bed you fell into the door of the bathroom. But it provided the essentials, it was available and it was cheap. We had a wonderful time. One evening we splurged and went for dinner and a dance to the fanciest hotel in town, the Imperial. On our first trip back to England 17 years later we stayed at the Imperial Hotel with great pleasure.

One our wedding day, December 11, 1944

For the first time since emigration I actually felt quite rich then. Not only was I on American officer's pay, which went a long way in wartime England, but my pay was boosted by the extra hazard pay which airborne soldiers got. I think for airborne officers, like myself, it was an extra $150 per month. While this may not seem much in today's money, it was a lot then and was a lot more in view of the fact that you didn't need any of it for everyday life. Quarters, uniforms and meals were supplied by the Army, as well as all needed health care and transportation. All money paid to us was essentially money to be saved. Of course many soldiers and officers blew much of that money on drink and gambling but those of us not so inclined could save it all. After three days in Torquay, we returned to London on the 14th for a second wedding ceremony, a Jewish ceremony performed by a Catholic U.S. Army chaplain. He did very well. That was part of his training and he did it cheerfully.

We had hoped to have a few more days together, but on the 17th or 18th we heard about the German breakthrough in the Ardennes, and the pilot who had flown me to England and I telephoned and decided that we had better get ourselves and our plane back to the Division in Reims.

When we landed in Reims, we found that this was once again only "82nd Rear" and the fighting units of our Division had left on an emergency mission further north. I was given orders to proceed north towards Belgium and to try to maintain radio contact with Division Headquarters for further direction. So a driver and I set out in a Jeep. The road was an endless convoy of trucks and jeeps and tanks heading in the same direction. Sometimes our Jeep was able to pass, but mostly we were hemmed in by this slow procession, moving day and night. We would have been a wonderful target for German dive bombers, but the same adverse conditions that prevented our Air Force from slowing the German advance also protected us that day. We went through village after village and town after town, much of it under blackout conditions.

In the dark, my driver and I may well have passed through Bastogne in our Jeep, though we didn't know the names of the towns we passed. The 101st Airborne Division was moving up in trucks at just about the same time. They were ordered to hold Bastogne at any cost. It was a crossroads the Germans needed on their drive westward. The 101st Airborne made a heroic stand at Bastogne, a major obstacle to the Germans rushing further west. Eventually, tired and worn out we caught up with our Division's Headquarters somewhere near a place called Trois Ponts, on the northern shoulder of he German breakthrough and they directed us to the forward headquarters of the 325th. That was the end of my honeymoon trip. Surely few can beat it for its range of extremes.

The Battle of the Bulge was Germany's brilliantly conceived, heavily supported and last ditch attempt to fight the Allies to a stand still and a negotiated peace. They had in great secrecy amassed all available reserves at a point in the front where the Allies—rightly, based on logic—least expected a massive counter attack. Their aim was a surprising and daring fast sprint by elite Panzers through the Ardennes to Liege and, ultimately, to relieve the German troops still hanging on to Antwerp. This would split the Americans in the South from the British in the north and deprive both of the hope of shortly taking the best harbor for resupply. While even Hitler could not have thought that this would bring victory, it was not unreasonable for him to think that it might bring the Allies to the negotiating table, his arguments reinforced by hoped for Allied fears of a Russian sweep deep into Western Europe. The release of German troops from the West to the East, which such an agreement would bring, could relieve that perceived fear.

They fully achieved the surprise, overran the lightly defended Ardennes front, poured troops in the resulting "Bulge", and their spearheads drove with great speed and ruthlessness toward Liege. They did not expect the quick and effective Allied response: two crack Airborne divisions committed on a day's notice, one, the 82nd, to help the British defend Liege and hold the northern flank of the Bulge in check, and the other, the 101st, to prevent the spearheads from passing through the essential road junction at Bastogne. Nor did they expect that Patton's powerful and heavily armored Third Army facing east could in so short a time wheel 90° to the north and so quickly attack the southern flank of the Bulge and relieve Bastogne.

That is the situation I drove into as I rejoined my division south of Liege. Then followed the worst weeks of the war for me. The Germans were known to have deployed elite English-speaking units clothed in American uniforms to spread confusion. This made my and my men's German accents dangerous. Our GIs were trigger happy. We were under injunction from our commanding officer to stay within the limits where we were known. Second, there was deep snow on the ground and we had to sleep in foxholes in the snow and mud. It was cold and miserable. Third, we were under almost constant artillery fire. Day in and day out and throughout the night shells landed haphazardly among us, causing serious casualties even at Regimental Headquarters level. The combination of being cold and wet and being shot at is not a good one. The nights in particular were miserable and scary.

Yet, once again I must emphasize that what I suffered was nothing compared to the front line troops who lived in equally miserable or worse foxholes but were, in addition to artillery fire, exposed to machine gun and small arms fire, had to go on nightly patrols to feel out where the enemy was, and were constantly subject to being attacked, overrun and killed by the still advancing Germans. My small intelligence unit was extremely busy, because a large amount of material that was important came through our lines and we were the first to interpret it. There was enormous confusion during the Battle of the Bulge. Nobody knew where the Americans were and where the Germans were, nor what German units were moving in what direction and what their strength was. The whole thing had come as a total surprise in a sector which the generals thought was the least likely to be attacked. Just how we missed the enormous concentration of men and armor in the weeks before is hard to fathom. It was one of several huge strategic intelligence failures on our side. We were much too cocksure of ourselves and of our having won the war and only having mopping up left to do to take the warnings that did filter through seriously.

It was also the first time that we were without air cover. We had become so used to air superiority, that being unable to communicate with fighter bombers overhead and directing them to targets we had identified was a new and unpleasant experience. The reason for this was that the visibility was terrible. The Air Force was grounded.

At one point when we were holding the shoulder of The Bulge near a town called Werbemont and the Germans were still driving west, our strategic mission was to keep the German armor from reaching Liege. One night one of our patrols ran into and captured alive the German Adjutant of a regiment of the 2nd S.S. Panzer Division. He was riding in a motorcycle side car. He had on him the 2nd SS Panzer's detailed plans for the next few days, which included their routes to Liege and on towards Antwerp. My men and I were the first to understand the significance of that capture. It proved of great help to our superiors. All our training and existence paid off generously that day. We were delighted and were commended, though the real commendation and medals went, as they should have, to the patrol that captured that officer and his driver alive.

Contrary to most of my American buddies, whose families were safe, I worried quite a bit at this time about Herta's safety in London. There was little German bombing by then; we had control of the air, but German "doodlebugs", the first unmanned missiles of any war, had begun to wreak havoc over London. They were mysterious as well as dangerous. I worried about her, and she about me, and both for food reason. As it turned out we were both lucky, neither the first nor the last time in our lives.

Then came New Years Day, 1945. We woke up to a cold, clear sky for the first time since the battle had started. Virtually every British and American combat plane in Europe must have been in the air over the Bulge that day. It was a gorgeous and encouraging sight, and it ended any hope of the Germans to get much further west. Antwerp, their target, was now clearly out of reach. Our fighter bombers were strafing every road and path where a German could be seen. But the fight was far from over. The German troops in the Bulge were fanatical. Driving them back through the mountains and woods of the Ardennes in deep snow was hard. We took heavy casualties and life was miserable for the two months or so that it took to reconquer the Bulge. We had to fight every inch of the way back to the Roer River

The Battle of the Bulge was over, but it had taken 80,000 American casualties, 16,000 killed. German losses were much heavier than that. Yet after two months, the front line was just about back where it had been. Nothing had been accomplished by this. The Germans' last mad adventure had got them nothing other than the final exhaustion of all their reserves, while American reserves were still pouring into Western Europe. By its end the outcome of the War in the West was no longer in question. I say the Germans' rather than, as it is often put, Hitler's last great battle. The reason is that, while it was Hitler's idea and he had to pressure his Generals to accept his plan, once it was decided it was brilliantly and fanatically executed by hundreds of thousands, ranging from the Generals in command to the Colonels leading the tank spearheads to the common soldiers advancing with enormous will and ingenuity through miserable terrain and hard opposition. We interrogated the captured ones and know how fanatical these soldiers still were.

Around the middle of February, 1945, our precious airborne division was pulled out of the front lines and went back into Theater Reserve near Reims and a relatively easy life. We received replacements for those who had been killed and wounded. They had to be trained. There was constant talk about an airborne drop across the Rhine. We got ready to board our planes a couple of times expecting to take off, but it was always canceled in the last minute. At some point there came the fortuitous taking of the Remagen Bridge by an advanced platoon of the Third Army, and thus the Rhine was breached.

There was one more airborne operation, and it was a drop across the Rhine north of us in the Second British Army sector. Just why Montgomery sacrificed airborne troops at a time when crossing the river was a given is beyond all of us, but a British airborne division, I think it was the 6th, did drop on the German side of the Rhine. A new untried American airborne division, the 17th, may also have been involved. I mention it here mainly because this is the operation in which Manfred Hertzog was killed. He was the son of Walter and Ceci Hertzog. I have described in Chapter I my finding Ceci Hertzog in Kassel after the War, when that poor woman who had survived Auschwitz had to learn not only that her husband was killed in the ovens of Auschwitz, but that her son, whom she believed safe in England, had enlisted in the British paratroop regiment and had lost his life in one of the last serious operations of the War

We had the privilege of enjoying life in Theater Reserve, at our base camps near Suippes and Sissonne, suburbs of Rheims, from the middle of February until April 1st. Although I have mentioned it before, this reminds me to emphasize once again the great advantage we had over the line infantry divisions. Veteran sergeants and junior officers in those divisions who had survived Normandy and the battle through France, the Battle of the Bulge and the advance to the Rhine, really knew that they had virtually no chance to survive intact. Sooner or later the law of averages would catch up with them. All around them were constantly new faces, replacements for fellow soldiers they had lost. In our division, once you survived a couple of months of the toughest combat, you had time to recoup and enjoy yourself and, though further operations were likely, the net turnover was less and the chance of survival seemed much greater. I think this had a lot to do with the incredible morale of the 82nd Airborne.

Well known entertainers of the time often came to entertain the troops. Some came to the two or three day rest areas just behind the front. Many more came when we were further back in reserve, such as at Reims. Ingrid Bergman frequently visited our Division. She was friendly with General Gavin. I had adored her for a long time. At one dinner dance, it may have been in the officer's mess at Reims, I pulled up all my courage and asked her to dance; a highpoint of my war.

In early April we moved by train and truck to Cologne. The city had already been taken by the 86th Division, from which we took over about thirty miles of Rhine River front.

Miraculously—or, perhaps, by design though such accuracy in bombing is hard to believe—the enormous gothic cathedral, the Dom, was left standing and virtually unhurt. I remember going into the Dom and looking at it, the only building preserved in that area as far as the eye could see, and as I was walking back to my Jeep across the large open square in front of the Dom, I heard a broadcast from another Jeep that I passed to the effect that Franklin Delano Roosevelt had died. I shall never forget the shock and disbelief that this caused, not only for me but virtually everybody else in our army. That evening the Division stood in formal formation, something that hadn't happened in months of combat, and had a parade and a service in memory of the late President whose indomitable spirit and intelligence and daring had brought us to what we then knew was victory just around the corner.

In front of the Cologne cathedral
the day President Roosevelt died, April 1944

Now for the first time, but continuing until the end of the War four weeks later, our small front line intelligence unit was probably the busiest in the entire Division. As the responsible officer, I got very little sleep. We were needed to interpret for higher officers, to interrogate prisoners brought in by aggressive patrolling across the Rhine River and for help with setting up the first military government units in Germany. There was an enormous pocket of German Army strength, the so-called "Ruhr Pocket", still across the river from us and higher headquarters was insatiable in its quest for intelligence as to just who they were and how good they were. At one point, one of our parachute regiments established a bridgehead across the river, principally to take prisoners and to get that sort of information. The Germans thought it was a major river crossing and threw the book at that bridgehead. It was withdrawn during the night. What it produced in intelligence materials passed through our hands and was considered very valuable by higher headquarters.

I just remembered that at that time we also helped produce German-language leaflets to be dropped by our artillery reconnaissance planes, Piper Cubs, over the German lines urging them to surrender. We even set up loudspeakers over which we German-speakers urged the same thing. That was real fun.

Near the end of April we got orders to move by train and truck north, once again to help the British 2nd Army spearhead its drive across the north-German plains, the very drive that we had hoped to enable six months earlier by our taking the Dutch bridges across the Rhine. Now the War, even in the front lines, became almost fun. Our front line units mostly rode on tanks of the American 7th Armored Division or on British armor down German roads, shooting at whatever looked suspicious. Resistance was generally only sporadic. Much of the German army then facing us consisted of relatively newly formed units of pitifully young and old men. The old ones looked for opportunities to surrender to us, knowing the Russians were at their heels. The thousands of 16 and 17-year-olds presented us with quite another problem. They had grown up in the Hitler Youth and to them Hitler's daily commands to stop us at any cost were gospel. They were fanatical even this late in the War and we took casualties cleaning them out. By this time even our troopers had become cautious. The war in Europe was won and nobody wanted to be the last casualty of that war. There was as a consequence a peculiar mixture of hate and pity on our side when we had to deal with these kids. They were so young, untrained and ineffective, yet they could and did kill ruthlessly and, contrary to their elders, remained defiant and had to be handled carefully even as prisoners.

Our little intelligence unit remained very busy. We were in great demand not only to interpret language, but also to give some background and advice involving the customs and character of the civilians and army units we were beginning to overrun.

Yet we reached the Elbe River with incredible speed and, in order to not let the fleeing Germans rest, immediately established bridgeheads on the other side of the river, though our troops were dead-tired. On the other side of the Elbe we began to overrun German Army rear installations, including hospitals and fuel dumps. The people there were flabbergasted to see us. They thought they were supporting front line troops facing east, the Russians. When they realized what had happened, they were most anxious to surrender to us, rather than wait for the Russians.

The Germans were very scared of being taken prisoner by the Russians. The Russian soldiers, like their entire country, had suffered terrible losses during a long brutal war which the Germans had started. They were in no mood to be kind and correct with their prisoners. They were also themselves short of supplies, lived largely off the land which they had occupied and had little to share with prisoners, even if they had been in a mood to do so. The Allies, on the other hand, could be relied on not to let their prisoners go hungry. The Germans' choice, given the opportunity to choose, was obvious.

At one point during these days a German general handed me with a flourish his silver plated pistol as a gesture of surrender. When I looked at it, I saw to my surprise that it was an American Army issue Colt .45 which he must have taken off some American and then later had it silver plated. That man had a very rough interrogation by me which he kept protesting was improper for a general. I felt otherwise. I still have that pistol, covered by an Army souvenir certificate.

On another day at the beginning of May Division Headquarters received two officers from the Command Staff of the Twenty-first German Army. They conveyed the desire of their commander, General von Tippelskirch, to surrender his rear echelon troops to the Americans, but only to the Americans. I was there with some other German-speakers. General Gavin laughed at them and said to go home and tell their general that we would accept only unconditional surrender of his entire Army, forward and rear. Otherwise, he said, we would drive on the next morning until we met the Russians and ground his Army to pieces. At that point, there may have been ten miles between our front lines and those of the Russians. That evening, May 2nd, General von Tippelskirch arrived in person. This time, he wanted to negotiate about surrendering his entire Army, approximately 150,000 men and their equipment, to the Americans. Once again he was told that only unconditional surrender was acceptable and that it would cover only such of his troops as may cross the American lines. General Gavin in clipped language told the German general that the Russians were our allies, that they had helped us win the War and we would not accept any condition that distinguished between Americans and Russians. General Gavin was quite moving in the speech he made to von Tippelskirch. That evening at about 10:00 PM von Tippelskirch surrendered his entire army to the 82nd Airborne Division, unconditionally and with a special clause making clear that the surrender covered only those troops that crossed the American lines and that those that might be overrun by the Russians belonged to the Russians. It was a grand moment for all of us in that house in Ludwigslust. 150,000 being surrendered to a division of roughly 17,000.

Our troops began to fraternize with the German girls, naturally, when we bivouacked overnight in some town or other. This was against the law but it was tolerated. Once again, the C-rations in every GIs pocket and the occasional bar of Hershey chocolate worked wonders, as did cigarettes.

Our war ended when our advance elements met the Russians outside a town called Ludwigslust, an important crossroads. The great day was marred because that day we also ran into the small but horrible concentration camp, called Woebbelin. I was with the first people there. The stench alone was so strong that the protestations of the Ludwigslust inhabitants to the effect that they knew nothing of what went on were obviously laughable. There were hundreds of dead bodies in the striped concentration camp uniforms stacked up several meters high and deep, and clearly visible through the barbed wire. There were also hundreds of almost starved to death people in it. Our colonel immediately asked the division commander to come down and see this, and Jim Gavin and his staff were there within a few minutes. One did not yet know about Auschwitz and Bergen-Belsen then. This was new to us. Interestingly enough, it cured our GIs at least for some time from having any relationship with the Germans. We had the obvious problems of not knowing how to feed these people. Would they die if we gave them our army chow? Division asked for instructions from higher headquarters and they sent some medical people down who in turn I don't think knew what to do but improvised and we began feeding and delousing and showering these people. How did we do that? By driving virtually every German out of every nearby house and taking it over for these people. The next day, following instructions from higher headquarters, we told the mayor of Ludwigslust to bring out the entire population, consisting mainly of women and old men and young children. We paraded them at gunpoint past the bodies, facilities and survivors. Then we had them dig graves in the most beautiful place we could find around there, the estate of the Duke of Mecklenburg. Men, mostly old, and women of the town were forced to place the dead bodies into those graves. Many of them threw up and thought that they couldn't do it. But our guns pointed menacingly and there was no doubt in anybody's mind that our troops meant business. Indeed, recalcitrant people were made to feel the butts of rifles, a reminder of how the Germans had acted earlier. I don't think that anyone who was involved in any way with the Ludwigslust concentration camp will ever forget it.

The inhabitants of Ludwigslust being made to
file past the dead of the concentration camp 1945

The funeral was attended by most of the soldiers, all of the top brass of the Division and by every man, woman and child of Ludwigslust. Our Division chaplain made a memorable speech on this occasion. I still have the text.

Of course, we German speakers were deeply involved in all of this. We were not kind or gentle with a mayor who said he had no idea that this was going on near his town. We began to collect names that we thought might later come in useful if there were a war crimes trial.

The concentration camp was horrible, but nothing, nothing on earth, could really dampen our spirits at that point. The war was over for us, we had won and we had survived. We were delirious. There was much celebrating and in general the mood was very, very upbeat. Of course, the war in the Far East was still going and the expected invasion of Japan would be murderous, we thought. The airborne troops might well be asked once again to spearhead that invasion. But that was far off in time and place, and we lived in the present, a time to be joyous.

For the Russians, too, this was a time to celebrate. We, of course, established liaison with the Russians and began partying with them. They had lots of vodka. We had trucks full of brandy taken in Normandy and champagne from Reims. So the liquor flowed freely and we truly enjoyed these initial contacts with the Russians. We German-speakers were in great demand because nobody on our side spoke Russian or on the Russian side spoke English, but a good many Russians could speak some German and understood German quite well. Therefore, I was often the chosen translator from English to German and back again. It assured that I was invited to the best parties.

I remember one sad incident which my linguistic skills got me into, which revealed quite a bit about the Russian army and the iron discipline that had got it to this point. An American soldier reported to one of our battalion headquarters that he had been held up at gunpoint by a Russian MP directing traffic at a crossroads, and had been forced to give up his watch, and then let go. The Battalion Commander thought that he ought to report this incident to his Russian counterpart, a Cossack Brigadier. So he asked the GI and me to come along in his Jeep to the Russian headquarters. I translated as best I could and the Russian general understood. He said "Come along, let's see if we can find the man." So we all rode to the crossroads and there, our soldier said, was the Russian MP still directing traffic. The General got out of his Jeep, walked up to the MP and spoke to him in Russian. Then we saw him pull out his revolver and shoot the man dead at point blank range. Then he came back grinning and said, "That's what we do with thieves in our army." Undoubtedly, he wanted to impress us. We were shocked to the core but there was nothing we could do. All this for a lousy GI watch.

I should say that in general our troops during the war had been quite good in their handling of prisoners. They were rough but they seldom were real ugly with prisoners. I do remember at one junction in the Ardennes seeing about a half dozen Germans in American uniforms with their throats cut. I was told that our paratroopers did that when they came across these imposters. They had been taught to kill by any means, including bayonets. After seeing enough of war, its brutality can become commonplace and accepted as a mode of life.

4. WITH U.S MILITARY GOVERNMENT OF GERMANY

Those days and weeks, however, consisted of more than just celebrations. I remember that we worked very hard. The confusion of having 150,000 armed Germans pass through our lines to prison camps, of having to disarm them and control them and direct them was enormous. But there were not only Germans going to prison camps, prison camps that were yet to be established. There were also DPs (Displaced Persons), concentration camp survivors and forced laborers from Poland and the Balkan States who had to be segregated from the Germans and for whom DP camps had to be established. Then there were freed Allied prisoners who had left prison camps and walked westward. They had to be processed. It became an administrative nightmare, for all these people not only had to be controlled and directed, they also had to be fed. The demands on us German-speakers and experts on the German Order of Battle were endless.

At the Potsdam Conference it was decided that Berlin would be divided into four sectors, an American sector, a British sector, a French one and a Russian sector. The Russians, of course, were occupying all of Berlin at the end of the war. Then orders came from up on high that the 82nd Airborne had been selected as the American Division to take over the American sector of Berlin from the Russians. This, of course, was a great honor and quite exciting, particularly for me. I was among the first hundred or so American officers going to Berlin to plan the takeover. I was enormously busy making arrangements for this major move. It was a fascinating time. Eventually, the bulk of our division arrived by truck, though a small group of paratroopers made a showy jump into Tempelhof Airport. I think this was solely to impress the Russians.

Berlin at this time was one huge pile of rubble. Only few houses still stood, and those were badly damaged. In the center of town nothing was standing. For our headquarters, we had to go to the suburbs around the Wannsee to find buildings that were still usable. Most of them were fancy villas of Party people and industrialists. Even they were damaged but habitable. Many of them had once upon a time been the villas of Jewish Berliners. Once again, we made short shrift of any Germans who still occupied such buildings, paying little regard to sex or age or health. They were simply kicked out into the streets from one minute to the next. Not nice, not considerate, but that's the way it was.

We immediately put guards around the ruins of Hitler's Chancery and various other German ministries. One couldn't go in, but we felt sure that important intelligence material would be buried under those ruins and we didn't want anyone else to get to it first. This proved to be a smart move. Much of the material later used in Nuremberg was recovered from those ruins.

I did not only do official tasks. I began to get letters from Herta and others through the Army mail asking me to search for certain people who might have survived. For example, I was successful in finding the brother and his wife of Nore Astfalck, of Stoatley Rough fame, and began to deliver food packages to them regularly. Similarly, I found portions of the family of Herta's old school friend, Gabi Landsberg, her brother and his daughter, in a miserable basement room. They were half Jewish and had survived. There were others more remote to whom I delivered food and clothes and other necessities, for the civilian population had almost nothing to eat then.

In Berlin 1945

Berlin in those days was a weird place. The Germans were in rags, without homes and starving. The Russian soldiers and officers, who had not been paid for most of the war, were now paid in "Occupation Marks". We, too were paid in Occupation Marks, and we could exchange those marks for dollars and deposit them in any American bank. It was impossible to tell whether the source of those marks was American, English, French or Russian. The Russian troops got so much money, which the Russians simply printed, that they carried it around in rucksacks full of paper money. The trading that went on was crazy. The Russians liked watches particularly. The bigger they were and the louder they ticked the better they liked them. Black faces got the highest prices. Virtually every American who had a watch sold it at that time for anywhere between $60 and $100. A black faced thick pocket watch would easily bring $300. Army issue underwear also was at a premium. There weren't many Americans at that time in Berlin who wore underwear under their uniforms. The black market flourished. Of course it was all relatively harmless so long as it was limited to the few things we had. However, it didn't take long for Air Force operators to begin flying in cases full of watches. At that point, the Army began to crack down, because cashing in the Russian money was becoming a serious drain on the American treasury. There was still a black market, of course, but it became illegal and being caught at it was costly.

Speaking German and having a Jeep and a driver at my disposal, I traveled all over Berlin and did a lot of exploring. The Wannsee Yacht Club had been turned into an Officer's Club. We found sailboats intact and went sailing on the lake. It was a wonderful time full of a sense of optimism and invincibility. There was no danger around. I don't know of a single American soldier who was attacked by Germans during this time in Berlin.

Prisoner interrogation went on, of course. We were beginning to ask a lot of questions about concentration camps. The invariable answer we got was that "We had no idea this was happening." This was so patently false that many times you just couldn't resist slapping the face of a person who said that and saying to him "Stop lying." Yet they insisted. They must have known, but except for those directly involved—which means hundreds of thousands—many of them just blocked it out and didn't want to know. However, it was obvious to us that thousands of people were involved in loading and driving and scheduling the trains that ran endlessly to the extermination camps, others were involved in the arrests and providing guards and the meticulous planning that went into the construction and erection of the camps and the extermination ovens. These people knew, and they were not just SS members. Most of them were civil servants and employees of companies and government agencies that did the dirty work.

There was also a lot of Army spit and polish once again, reminders of my Governors Island days. Important people came through day after day. I remember having an opportunity to admire the private B-17 of Averell Harriman, our Ambassador to Russia. I had never seen a plane until then with a bed and couches and easy chairs in it. Our Division paraded a great deal in white gloves and white leggings once again and put on great demonstration parachute jumps for dignitaries. It was the Army version of fun and games.

And there was even some cultural life. I shall never forget a performance of Brecht's "Three Penny Opera" in a bombed out theater without roof by starving German actors just off "Under den Linden", the wide representational thoroughfare leading to the Brandenburg Gate. Through the broken windows we could see an endless procession of homeless people pushing carts full of pitiful belongings. The happenings on the stage took on frightful reality. We were living in the midst of all the hunger, venality and humanity of that play.

At some point during this period I managed to dream up a reason for orders to go to Western Germany. I took my Jeep and drove west to Hanover and then south into country I remembered well as I approached Kassel. It was an emotion-charged trip. The town was completely in ruins. But I drove endlessly around its streets, found our house which was bombed to bits. I drove down to the Fulda where I used to keep my boat and I drove up to the hills above Kassel where I used to ski. I didn't encounter a single person whom I recognized. Then I drove out towards the little village of Ihringhausen, where Ida, the woman who had raised my sister and me and stuck with us through thick and thin, had lived when we last heard of her and lo and behold, I found her. As I have previously mentioned, it was a moving and wonderful reunion. She cried at the pleasure of seeing me again in one piece, an American officer, and hear the news of my family. She could not hear enough. We had a perfectly wonderful time and I saw to it that she was supplied with enough food to carry her through the next few weeks. I promised to stay in touch.

Then, almost by instinct, I drove into the western suburbs of Kassel where I surmised some of the old villas might have survived, including, perhaps, that of Dr. Fritz Blumenfeld, the doctor and pediatrician, whose life and miserable end at the hands of the Nazis I have described in Chapter 1. His widow, who was not Jewish, could have made it. And yes, she did! But not only was she at the good old "House Heimgarten", but here I found also Ceci Hertzog, a good friend and distant relative of my family. She turned out to be one of the relatively few who survived Auschwitz, She had made her way to Kassel and, just like myself, sought and found Leni Blumenfeld in her country house. What a reunion! But, as mentioned before, the pleasure of being the first to find these two women was, unfortunately, tempered by the fact that not only had Ceci Hertzog's husband been killed in the concentration camps but, even worse, her young son whom they had managed to get out of Germany to England in one of the last transports of children from Germany to England, had been killed as a soldier in the British Army during the last few weeks of the war. My ability to give these two women news of those of the family abroad about whom I knew was, of course, a great pleasure to them. In reverse, I was able to inform the rest of the family of their survival and whereabouts and was also able to assure that they would have plenty to eat at a time when many of the Germans around them were starving.

Leni Blumenfeld, Hans and Ceci Herzog
in Kassel 1944

Herta and I had been in touch, mainly by mail but occasionally I managed to fight my way through the Army telephone system to some London headquarters, and then sweet-talked an English army operator to connect me with her civilian number in London. That was against regulations but fun and exciting. When on late night duty in some dugout in Belgium with lots of time to kill and little enemy action, the game was not just to get through to London but to try to do it in the most round-about way possible: from Battalion Headquarters to Regiment, then Division, then Corps, then Army, then Army Group, then Theater, then from European Theater HQ to North Africa, and thence to the Pentagon and back to London. The trick was that you had to know the supposedly secret code name of each headquarters. We had a passion for collecting those codes, which could be helpful also in other more legitimate enterprises. Obviously, what we did—and I was not the only one—constituted an outrageous tying up of phone lines, but oh how satisfying to hear Herta's faint voice at the end of that long chain!

Anyway, mail and phone contact was no longer good enough. We really wanted to live together now as soon as we could and we tried to find ways of doing it. In the Fall of 1944 Herta discovered that the American Army was recruiting German-speakers for work with the Army in Germany, mainly in a mail censorship role. I told her to try to get in and she did. She was issued a uniform and transported to a collection point in Paris. So what did I do? Once again I managed to get myself temporary duty orders to proceed to Paris—you had to have good friends in the Personnel section of your division, and I did—and I proceeded in a long non-stop drive from Berlin to Paris by Jeep. It was strenuous and slow, because the roads were bad and there was a great deal of military traffic, French, British and then American. Eventually, I found my way to the part of Paris where Herta was supposed to be but, just as when I arrived in England for our wedding, she was not to be found. I was tired and exhausted but I searched. I knew that Herta's family had some family connections in Paris, whom she was anxious to find. So I pursued her from point to point and, eventually, we caught up with each other. It was a wonderful reunion, the first since our foreshortened honeymoon and the first after months during which my survival was far from certain. We saw a lot of Paris together joyously in each other's company.

Herta in Paris in American uniform 1945

Eventually, I had to return to my post in Berlin. The open question at that point was: where are they going to send Herta. However, since she was now in the European Theater of Operations and within the Army's communication system, the chances were good that we could communicate by telephone. Eventually, I learned that she had been assigned to Munich, and once she got there, I was given her precise address at a former SS encampment at Pullach outside Munich.

What I had to do now was clear. Somehow, I had to get myself transferred to Munich, which meant leaving my fascinating job in Berlin and, even more importantly, leaving the 82nd Airborne. It may be hard for anyone who has not lived through combat with an elite outfit to understand the deep emotional attachment to what after all is an abstract concept, an Army division. And yet, there it was, it was hard to think of leaving it voluntarily.

Moreover, round about this time we learned that the 82nd Airborne Division had been selected to lead the great VE victory parade planned for New York. We were clearly considered The Elite Outfit in the U.S. Army at that point. Naturally, I would also have loved to have been part of that great show, but Herta's draw was even stronger.

So, once again, I had to get myself temporary duty orders, this time to Munich. This was a lot easier, of course, for an intelligence officer then it was for one of the line officers. I could always think of something that needed to be done at some intelligence headquarters, near where I wanted to go. So I once again proceeded in my Jeep from Berlin to Munich. I stopped in Kassel for a second time. Somehow, I got special pleasure out of driving around that city in ruins and of visiting Leni Blumenfeld and Ceci Hertzog in their small villa outside Kassel. They spoiled me with good cooking, and I spoiled them with supplying the ingredients for that and many more meals from the local Army PX.

Through them I learned that another old friend of my family, Leni Gross, had managed to survive the war in Paris and had returned to Kassel to reclaim her grandfather's factory. I located her and found her in the beginnings of an extraordinary enterprise. She must have been in her late twenties at that point. About ten years earlier she had caused a great scandal in Kassel when she eloped with a young Arab from, I believe, Beirut. That marriage did not last long. He wanted to add her to his harem and she managed to escape. However, through this marriage she had acquired French citizenship and, therefore, was able to establish residence in Paris rather than return to Nazi Germany. How she survived as a Jew in Paris I don't know, but she did.

She was a tiny unattractive woman but of enormous willpower and determination. Her grandfather's large factory that had produced textile products, mostly canvas for tents and the like, I believe, was, of course, in ruins. She aggressively pursued the restitution of this property to her, way ahead of the laws later passed in Germany for such restitutions and, more importantly, forced the Germans to give her the manpower and materiel to rebuild the factory way ahead of any other German rebuilding. She became the president of the company and ran it with an iron fist. Being one of the few factories producing anything in Germany at that point, it was enormously successful. She became rich and, eventually, bought the most elegant residence in and around Kassel, namely, the official guest house of what had been Kassel's largest industry, the Henschel Locomotive Works, owned by the Henschel family mentioned in Chapter I. I think it gave her special pleasure to live in the luxurious place which many top Nazis had also occupied. Herta and I visited her there repeatedly. She died in her early sixties.

After this interesting stop, I went to Munich where the Office of Military Government for Bavaria was then just beginning to establish itself. It was not difficult for me to find a place that needed a German-speaking officer. There were several such places, but I chose the de-nazification branch. The major in charge of that branch offered to try to requisition me through channels, and that was the best I could do. For the next few days, Herta and I could enjoy each other's company until I had to return to Berlin—another very long Jeep drive.

It took some doing getting the transfer approved through channels before my division left for New York, but it worked. I took leave from lots of wartime friends and then proceeded to Munich.

At this point, I may well have been the first American officer in the Occupation Forces who was actually married to a woman stationed in the same town. There was no precedent for giving us appropriate quarters. However, we had set so many precedents already, we managed to deal with that issue quite well. At first I was assigned to officer quarters with other intelligence personnel, where Herta and I only had our own room. This was in the middle of Munich in a large stone house, one of the few habitable places. Subsequently, we moved into our own apartment on the fourth floor of a restored apartment building about 20 minutes by car from the center. Much later we managed to move into a very nice two story villa with a conservatory and a big garden in Harlachin, a suburb of Munich, that had belonged to a Nazi dentist, who was unceremoniously kicked out.

Then came a wonderful year for both of us. Every morning, Herta went to her work by Army bus, and I went to mine either with a driver picking me up or, later, in a requisitioned two-door BMW coupe that was assigned to me. We worked during the week and on weekends enjoyed the Bavarian and Austrian surroundings of Munich. In summer there were the lakes, near most of which the Army had established officers' recreational facilities in requisitioned hotels. You could stay there and eat there for next to nothing and have fun. We did.

In the winter there was skiing and a choice of many resorts. Garmisch-Partenkirchen, the largest German ski resort, had been taken over by the Army as a major recreation center. Every hotel and inn was available for little money, some to enlisted men, some for sergeants and some for officers. I had skied since I was about eight, but that was interrupted, first by Nazi anti-semitism, then by the absence of skiing in England, then by the lack of funds in America.

I can remember only one ski trip with some other refugee boys to Cannon Mountain in New Hampshire. I must have borrowed equipment from others who were better off than I. We had wooden skis and skins and spent the better part of the day hiking and "skinning" up the Cannon trail to the top. Then we ate our sandwiches on the top and skied down once. That was a typical day of skiing in those days. It didn't afford much chance to improve one's style—which still shows.

Herta in the snow in Bavaria 1946

In that first winter in Munich after the war I was determined to make up for lost time on skis, but Herta had never been on skis. So I—rashly as it turned out—undertook to teach her. The first couple of times went well and she picked it up satisfactorily. The third time we took the cog railway up to the top of the Zugspitze, Germany's highest mountain, not to ski down but to ski in the large and rather easy snow bowl below the Zugspitz Haus, the Army-run hotel at the peak. Way down in that bowl, while slowly snow plowing under my tutelage, Herta managed to fall forward. She had trouble getting up. I told her to do so anyway and "to step on it." She couldn't and was obviously in pain. What to do? There were no ski patrols, no lifts. The only means of transportation out of that bowl, other than climbing on foot, was by means of a wooden container on skids, that could be let down from the top by means of a rope controlled by a winch. That vehicle eventually got Herta and me back to the top, where there was a litter but no other medical attention. In pain, she had to wait all day for the 5 pm train to take us off that mountain peak.

As we learned later that day, the Army had a Field Hospital in Garmisch, at which it had concentrated the majority of orthopedic surgeons still in the Army at that time. They were competent enough, but their bedside manners left much to be desired. Herta may well have been the first female patient they had seen in years. They had also lost sympathy with most of their patients, many of them soldiers that had never been on skis, many of whom had hardly ever seen snow, who ignored all warnings and, on their Army issue skis, headed straight down the slopes at high speed and totally out of control. So the Major who looked at Herta's X-ray coolly informed us that she had a spiral fracture of both the tibia and the fibula, that she would have to be in a cast and off that leg for at least three months and that he couldn't promise that one leg would not be permanently shorter than the other. It was a discouraging prognosis.

Herta was transferred to the Army's 98th General Hospital in a former Catholic hospital in Munich, where most of the nurses were German nuns. She had a sunny room to herself and "Frau Oberleutnant", as she was addressed, soon took over running the ward. Later I had to carry her up many flights of stairs when we returned to our 4th floor apartment or went visiting.

The time passed quickly and, as I remember, quite pleasantly and, of course, her leg healed well and without any foreshortening. We even had two beautiful Irish setters for some months. They were a pleasure but, unfortunately, they were over bred by Germans eager to sell them to Americans, and disease-prone. They died.

Life was by no means all play. We took our Military Government duties seriously. I had a nice office. At my direction, the wall between me and the big room in which my people worked was taken out and replaced by a glass partition Then as now I liked to be in the middle of things. Activity around me has never kept me from being able to concentrate.

It was a motley crew that I chose to work for me. There were two or three non-refugee Americans with an investigative background and some command of German. Sergeants Graf's and Chernoff's names come back to me. Then there were some Polish-Jewish men from Displaced Persons camps and a very few Germans with convincing anti-Nazi credentials. For all such people, a job with Military Government meant not only pay but also the end of starvation for them and their families. We could be choosy.

All Germans who wanted to work in any position of responsibility in the German economy, or in any position for American organizations, had to fill out one of those then famous "Frageboden"—questionnaires, in which they had to report under oath all their positions, memberships and activities between 1925 and 1945. Our principal job was to investigate the truthfulness of the answers and, on the basis of the answers and our investigation, to recommend the classification of each person into one of three categories: Active Nazi, Nazi affiliated but not active, and Non-Nazi. The active Nazis were barred from anything but physical labor. The middle category had limited, carefully defined employability. Only the Non-Nazi category was fully employable. Sensitive jobs, like teaching were to be open only to the Non-Nazis. Where we found fraud in the Fragebogen we recommended prosecution. Fairly soon, tribunals were established to which Germans feeling aggrieved by the initial classification could appeal for "denazification". At times our investigators testified before these tribunals.

Among many other entities, we cleaned out the whole University of Munich, where only a small handful were non-Nazis and the vast majority were kicked out as active Nazis. We did other industrial concerns, the medical people at hospitals, and so on and so on. We thought we did valuable, lasting work that would help change the Germany of the future. Little did we anticipate that under the influence of the Cold War and the Allies' perceived need of Germany on their side, virtually all of our work was undone within about five years.

We were shocked by the predominance of active Nazis in the professions—lawyers, doctors, judges, teachers and university professors, and ranking civil servants. After all, these were the products of the once-thought-to-be-the-greatest German universities, where humanism had reigned. Should they, at least, not have known better? Unfortunately, they did not. The German universities, notwithstanding their high intellectual standards, also imbued most students with extreme nationalist and right-wing ideas, with a glorification of aggressiveness and fighting, with a sense of absolute obedience to those higher in the hierarchy, as well as an antisemitism deeply ingrained in history, particularly the history of the German universities. Of course, such a broad generalization never covers all. There had once been great humanists on the German university faculties, but, as we found, all of them had long since been removed by the Nazis. One of the real pleasures of our job was to find these people and reinstate them.

Herta was not enamored with her censorship work which, contrary to my work, was boring, although the group of German-speakers that she was a part of was an interesting one and a good many of them became good friends of ours. The majority were German refugees from England. We are still in touch with quite a number of them.

Herta continued with a vengeance, and on a much larger scale than I had in Berlin, the job of trying to find, and when found supply with food and other necessities, friends and relatives of people we knew in England and America. My influence as an American officer, and the availability to me of transportation, was helpful. Between us, we were extraordinarily successful. Eventually, this led to ties to the Munich office of the American Joint Distribution Committee, the big Jewish organization that took responsibility for the thousands of Jewish and partly Jewish Displaced Persons who were then being herded into DP camps all over Bavaria. One of the important things JOINT did was to establish a search bureau, which attempted to help the thousands of lone survivors who were trying to find out what happened to their families and friends. Eventually, Herta managed to transfer from the Army Censorship Bureau to becoming a JOINT employee involved in this search work. This was the kind of work Herta was born to do. Her networking instincts came into full play. It was useful, at times heart rending work which she did with great efficiency, inventiveness and success.

One of the "good" Germans who worked for me was Ferdinand Westerbarkey. He and his wife became friends. When their first son was born, we got them diapers and other baby supplies from America, things then totally unavailable to Germans, and we also helped feed them and supply other needs. Seventeen years later, when Herta and I undertook our first trip back to Europe, I asked Ferdinand, with whom we had stayed in touch, whether he could recommend a hotel near his house in Munich and a car rental agency. This was before Hertz and Avis had established themselves in Germany. His response was: "Stay with us and use one of our several cars and I will have my chauffeur pick you up." To make a long story short, Ferdinand Westerbarkey had become rich. My poor employee of

1945 had teamed up with a person who had invented a cheap way to make whiskey out of whey at a time when hard liquors were totally unavailable to Germans. He made a killing and then built the company into one of the great food import and export operations of post-war Germany. A wonderful success story for a deserving and imaginative German. His entire family became friends.

At some point round about this time I had been promoted to the rank of Captain. Life in the ETO as an American officer was both interesting and outrageously comfortable. When we did not feel like cooking for ourselves, we ate in the officers' mess. When we needed to buy something, we went to the Army PX. At both places we got first rate service and goods at ridiculously cheap prices. In fact, the officers mess was quite an elegant place: the "Haus der Deutschen Kunst", the very museum where the Nazis had once staged their infamous art show "Entartete Kunst", to ridicule the "Degenerate Art" of most of the best known artists of the 20th Century. We also had cars and, if wanted, drivers for those cars and weekend trips into the beautiful countryside around Munich were standard. We could stay at hotels reserved for Americans on the various Bavarian and Austrian lakes or on top of mountains. There, too, we got first rate treatment from the Germans who ran these places. They badly needed what they were paid to serve us and also wished to ingratiate themselves. We led the lives of "conquerors". Not slaves like those the Romans brought home, but something not so very far removed from that status was at our disposal.

The German-speakers in military government in particular felt so comfortable, that it was hard to decide to leave this good life. Even the pay we received was far better than at least those of us who had been refugees had ever envisaged. Yet Herta and I did a lot of talking among ourselves and with others about the future. At that time it looked as if, if we wanted to, we could stay on in important jobs in military government or other American agencies in Germany for years. On the other hand, what was the long term future? It was difficult to imagine going back after the heady life in Europe to being an assistant buyer of leather goods in New York. It would take years to reach an income level in such a job that would allow us to start a family. We decided to sign up for one more year with military government and the JOINT Distribution Committee, respectively, but to take a long leave in America during the Summer of 1946 to explore alternatives and later decide whether we should stay on in the ETO or start a new life in America. In that additional year I would be doing the same interesting military government job, but I would do it as a civilian employed by the Army, rather than as an Army Captain. I would still be in uniform and have an officer's privileges, but the pay would be much better—a real opportunity to save for the future.

There was another factor that made us hesitate about leaving. Herta, who had never been in the United States, was distrustful of what to expect and whether she could adapt to life there. Much of what she had seen and heard did not encourage her. An army is seldom a good advertisement of the best in a country. Yet, going back to England was out of the question. I could not get a work permit in post-war England. Moreover, England for years remained on food rations and suffering from the aftereffects of wartime shortages. The choice clearly was between making a career in the American services in Europe, where short range promise was great but the long range was uncertain, or to start a new life in the States.

We also began to consider a variant to returning to a job at Saks. America had passed the GI Bill of Rights, one of the most far sighted and productive pieces of legislation ever. It allowed returning veterans to attend any educational institution they chose at government expense, with enough of an additional allowance to permit a modest existence without other income. By that time I had had two years of night school at City College plus the various Army schools I had been sent to, including the three terms of Moroccan study at the University of Pennsylvania. It didn't amount to much. I could, of course, go home to go to college, but that meant a long haul of studying and with the future still unresolved when I graduated.

In military government, I was working with loads of American lawyers. I enjoyed working with them and intellectually found their approach to problem solving interesting. It came easily to me. This raised the possibility of trying to get into law school. Though it may be hard to believe, it is a fact that we were still almost totally ignorant of the American educational establishment. We had heard of Harvard and Yale Universities and not much more. Because of my legal contacts, I had also heard that Columbia University had a good law school. We decided to use our 1946 summer in the States to explore the law school possibility as well.

Joe Kaskell, last mentioned as my father's savvy lawyer in Berlin, played an important part in this decision. As previously mentioned, he had become an American lawyer and his wife, Lilo, a photographer, had managed to get a press assignment to occupied Germany early in 1946. He accompanied her and they came to visit us in Munich. We quickly established close rapport and I could be most helpful to both of them in accomplishing what they wanted to do in Germany. This led to their inviting us to be their guests on a trip to Switzerland, skiing in St. Moritz and staying at that most fabulous of hostelries, The Souvretta Haus. The four of us went together in my Army-assigned Horch Convertible. It was a wonderful trip. In the course of it, Joe and Lilo became good, older friends and advisors to us. Joe himself, an accomplished German lawyer, chose to become an American lawyer after he emigrated and in his mid-40s started all over again by going through the full three years at Columbia Law School. I think he overlapped with his son Peter at Columbia Law. Joe strongly urged me to apply to law school and not to give up on account of my insufficient college background. He gave me good leads. We remained close to the Kaskells for the rest of their lives.

The next problem was how to get from the ETO to America and back. Going there was easy, though of course we could not do it together. I would get Army travel orders as an officer on leave. No problem. Herta could go as a "war bride". Ships full of war brides were going to the United States from England and France at this point. With millions of Americans in Europe, thousands and thousands of marriages with local girls had taken place, and the Army undertook to transport them to the United States. We could not in advance solve the problem of how to get Herta back to Munich for the extra year that we had committed ourselves to, but figured that somehow the problem could be solved. So, in June 1946, we departed on separate routes to the States. I went on a big American ship and had to sign all sorts of papers for Herta. I tried to be clever, too clever. Since we wanted to explore the United States that summer, I decided to "consign" Herta not to New York, where my mother was expecting us, but to friends in San Francisco. In that way, I hoped, the Army might pay for all or part of our planned trip across the country.

Herta's ship went first. My mother was there to pick her up in New York City, but, alas, the Army wasn't about to release her to an unknown woman not designated on Herta's "Bill of Lading". The Army was going to take her under guard to a train across the country to San Francisco. Then ensued an extended period of frantic cables going back and forth and resulting eventually in my being able to authorize the release of Herta into my mother's arms. By that time I should have known the Army and its way of adherence to the letter of whatever was on paper well enough not to have tried this gambit. On the other hand, I had been spoiled in the ETO. As an officer, you could talk your way in and out of almost anything if, but only if, you were there in person. And of course I was not on that pier in New York. However, it all ended well.

My mother, of course, was delighted to have us with her in New York that summer of 1946. It was about three years since my father had died. She was lonely, but never complained and had really made a life for herself which satisfied her. She had never been gregarious. Being on her own was not as much of a hardship to her as it might have been to others, I believe.

She and Herta got along very well, which was important to us and we were pleased that it worked. So was she. For Herta this summer meant getting accustomed to America: the heat of summer, the lights, the big cars, the abundance of food and of everything else. For the prior six years she had lived in wartime England, with food rationing and blackouts at night. Then there came our life in the ruins of Germany. And before that, at Stoatley Rough, life had also been frugal. The onslaught of American wealth and abundance was, in one way, wonderful to her but in the end she wasn't at all sure that greater happiness might not be found in less abundance. However, we explored with open eyes and open minds.

I had interviews at Harvard Law School, Yale Law School, and at Columbia. All expressed concern at my lack of an orderly college education and the degree which their brochures said was required. However, the interview at Harvard, with one of the all time greats of the Law School, Warren Seavey, went particularly well. We hit it off. Of course, I was in my captain's uniform with my Bronze Star and all my battle ribbons on my chest and colorful fourragères on both shoulders. Seavey, who had been in World War I, was interested in the details of my experience and asked perceptive questions concerning my background and how I reacted to the ups and downs of my earlier life and to the U.S. Army. He made no promises, but he also did not rule out the possibility of admission.

We liked what we saw of Boston. Old friends of my parents, Fritz and Emmy Lieberg, lived there and showed us around. The first drive along the Charles River impressed us, particularly all the sailboats out on the river and the stories Fritz told us about it all being free for everybody, including poor inner city kids.

I don't remember all the other things we did that summer. I do know we visited Joe and Lilo Kaskell and stayed with them in their summer place in Madison, New Hampshire. We arrived at their beautiful but remote place in the dark, banged on the door and were greeted by Joe with a shotgun at the ready. He thought our banging signaled the return of an unwanted visitor, the local porcupine, and was determined to put an end to the damage that animal was capable of doing. The gun was lowered promptly and we had the first of a good many wonderful visits to their retreat "On The Hill". Joe continued to take a great interest in my career and both Joe and Lilo in our lives and family. To jump ahead for a moment, much later, Joe tried to persuade me to join him in New York as his partner and, when he retired, to take over his practice. By that time I was too firmly established in Boston and Herta was too firmly of the view that one could not raise children in New York City for us to accept this otherwise very tempting offer.

One of the important things we accomplished that summer was to make Herta an American citizen within four weeks of her arrival in this country. Somewhere I found an obscure regulation which authorized immediate citizenship for foreign spouses of American government employees where the spouse was legally in this country but the American was under orders to return to government service abroad. It was tailor-made for us and it worked.

When my leave was up I returned to Germany. In those days, of course, one did not fly. It took seven or eight days on a boat, but in great comfort. The problem was how to get Herta back. Making her an American citizen was only the first step toward solving that problem. We were unable to solve it completely by the time I left and she had to pursue a lot of different possibilities on her own. Virtually all transatlantic transportation at the time was still controlled by the government and used to transport troops and troop-related people and materiel. There was no private travel. Of course, Herta had a job offer from the American JOINT Distribution Committee in her pocket. But they could not arrange transportation for her. In the end, she managed to get on a freighter out of Halifax. Thus, by the end of the summer, we were reunited in Munich living in great comfort in our villa in Harlachin

This final year with the U.S. Military Government in Germany is a blur in my memory. It was quite a wonderful time of comfortable living, interesting work, easy travel wherever we wanted to go and continuation of what seemed like an unending honeymoon for Herta and me. Cultural activity had revived in Germany. We went to the theater, the opera and many concerts.

Through Herta's work we got to know Frau Kleemann, a German woman who was married to a Jew who had emigrated with that last desperate group via Russia to Shanghai. Herta had received a request from the husband in China to find his wife. She did. She was a wonderful woman, but desperately poor and starving. We took her in and she became our house keeper, secretary and general helper. She spoiled us, and we her. We stayed in touch after we left, and were delighted when she was ultimately reunited with her husband in Germany.

Among the people we rediscovered for friends was Inge Hamburger's sister Suse, who had managed to survive as a half-Jew. We arranged a meeting of the two sisters at the Swiss border; Inge came to a prearranged spot on the Swiss side, and we drove Suse to the corresponding spot on the German side. The two could talk to each other but could not touch. This kind of enterprise was fun and made us feel that we were not only enjoying our privileged status but also used those privileges for the good of others. There was much of that sort of activity that could only be done safely if you were in American uniform and had the requisite passes and transportation.

Similarly, we made it possible for Nore Astfalck and Hannah Nacken to return to Germany at a time when no civilians from abroad were permitted to come to live in occupied Germany. They felt their work for refugee children in England was largely done and that their talents were now needed far more in the rebuilding of Germany. We succeeded and they immediately began amazing new careers, first as teachers at the reopened Odenwald Schule, an old private school with very liberal educational ideas that had been closed by the Nazis. They helped to reestablish it. Later they decided that they needed a bigger and less exclusive arena for their work. They took over the Immenhof, a large institution near Celle in Northern Germany, run by the Arbeiterwohlfahrt, a nation-wide social welfare organization closely allied to the newly reestablished Social Democratic Party of Germany. It was a big, spread-out place in the country to which mothers, alone or with children, came for convalescence, rehabilitation, reschooling and the like, a perfect place for Nore Astfalck as director to engage her superb organizational talents and ingenuity. Unfortunately, Hannah Nacken died not long after the two, who had been together a lifetime through thick and thin, came to the Immenhof. This was a hard blow for Nore. We visited her and she came to see us in Munich. Much later both our daughter Helen and Inge's daughter Nicole spent some weeks at the Immenhof as interns. It was good for their German, but they had some trouble living with Nore's autocratic tendencies. We never had any trouble with those. Was that thanks to our German upbringing or did she revert to more Germanic ways on her return? I don't know.

Though we did so many other things, my de-nazification work also continued apace during this time. It was not ignored. Our investigations brought to light more and more of the knowledge of Nazi times which, by now, is commonplace but in those days was largely new and virtually unbelievable. The War Crimes Trials in Nuremberg were taking place and I went there several times to listen. It was wonderful to see all of the surviving top Nazis, all who had not killed them-selves, in the dock as prisoners. The evidence presented was horrifying, but cre-ated an irrefutable record of the times for future generations. And new international law was made, which we are still trying to refine. It was a heady endeavor carried out by some of the best legal brains in the world.

The result of all this was that we learned to distrust almost every German born much before 1930. In our minds there was a presumption of guilt which only in a few cases was successfully overcome. In later life many second thoughts appeared, particularly the nagging question: what might we have done had we not been Jewish? But at that time, so close to the War and surrounded by evidence of terrible things having been done by people of our generation, we had no hesitation to apply the presumption of guilt universally.

Herta's work progressed and, in many ways, confirmed our attitude towards the Germans. She dealt day-in and day-out with survivors of concentration camps, their desperate efforts to find out what happened to spouses, parents, children and more remote relatives and the terrible news which she had to give to so many of them. On the other hand, she also was instrumental in reuniting dozens and dozens of these desperate people with loved ones. That was a great upside in her job. At one point, a Jewish Army chaplain and she faced the job of getting a group of over 100 DPs out of Germany. They ended up "requisitioning" an entire train and escorting those people on the train and out of Germany. Amazing things were possible then if you had some imagination and someone with some authority to assist you.

We continued to have fun on weekends at the wonderful Army installations all over Bavaria and Austria. We also during that year took trips by car over the Alps into Italy and past the North Italian lakes back into Switzerland. We saw Venice and Nice, loved Grasse and its surroundings in back of the French Riviera. We were among the privileged few tourists in those days. Hotels were empty and cheap. Everybody—but everybody—loved Americans then and as an officer in American uniform we were treated royally wherever we went, usually not for our money but for having won the War. These were still exhilarating times for us survivors, hard to imagine now.

We also met interesting people. The Heitans, for example, a French Jewish couple, he a doctor she a social worker, who had somehow survived in France. He had been a doctor in the French Resistance. She now was Herta's immediate boss at Munich JOINT and he gave medical help in the DP Camps. They had reclaimed their beautiful villa on the Riviera. They were both wise and lively and we loved being with them both in Munich and on our travels.

I have always been interested in cars and the occupation was no exception. In the early days, before things became organized, we found our cars in German garages and if they pleased us just took them. Eventually we were forced to turn them in to Army motor pools, from where—if you had friends in the right places—they were generally reassigned to you. That is how I got that lovely BMW two-seater coupe, I think a 1940 model, eight cylinders in line, that served me very well throughout our Munich stay and was a pleasure to drive. The Army maintained it for us. For trips with more people, I had an enormous Horch 12 cylinder convertible at my disposal. It must have weighed 5000 lbs or more and had the most melodious, exhaust-driven horn. That is the car that took the Kaskells and us to St. Moritz, just the right car to drive up to the Souvretta Haus in. Then American car manufacturers began to reconvert to civilian production and in 1946 Nash offered Occupation Army personnel their first post-war sedans on extraordinary liberal terms. I bought one, knowing that upon leaving Europe I would be able to sell it at a good profit, for such vehicles were still a rarity in Europe then. That is exactly how it worked out.

In the winter of 1946 I composed applications for admission to Harvard, Yale and Columbia Law Schools. I took a great deal of time and trouble doing this, to Herta's amusement. The investment of time and effort proved to have been worthwhile, for rather to our surprise both Harvard and Columbia were willing to have me without a college degree and at best two years of the equivalent of full time college. Once again, we were enormously pleased and excited and chose Harvard, knowing little about it other than that it was in Boston, which we, particularly Herta, greatly preferred to New York. How well that worked out!

In June of 1947 I left the Army for good, after five years, four years as an enlisted man and officer, and the last year as a civilian employee of military government. Contrary to many, I never hated army life. Though no one likes to be shot at or to live in snowbound foxholes, I rather flourished under Army discipline, learned my way around the U.S. Army and how to live at peace with it. It was also a priceless introduction for me, a German refugee, to America and Americans. After some time in the Army, I stopped feeling like a foreigner, as I had in England and in the first two years in America. I became an American in the U.S. Army.

Nor was it just the two of us, Herta and I, who were leaving the Army that June of 1947. Shortly before we left Germany we had learned that Herta was pregnant. There was another passenger, as yet unseen and unnamed but felt, who accompanied us on our way to our next great adventure: Law School and life in Cambridge, MA.

Herta and Hans with the new-born
Helen in Cambridge MA 1948

POSTSCIPT

Here ends the first phase of my life's Story, the part which, I believe, is intrinsically the most interesting and unusual. My life up to our arrival in Cambridge, Massachusetts, took shape in strange and historically important circumstances: my early days as a kid of typically emancipated and assimilated German Jews in a world which unbeknown to us was destined for an early and terrible oblivion; having to deal as an adolescent with personal and collective ostracism and the collapse of my parent's world; life as a refugee student in pre-War England and as a poor refugee immigrant in New York; almost five years in the U. S. Army preparing for war, taking part in major battles, and then deeply engaged in the transition from war to peace in occupied Germany. All these formed an inherently interesting background to my story, a unique era that will never recur in the same way.

In contrast, the rest of my story plays against a far more conventional background. After refugee life and The War, Harvard Law School was a profound experience that generated new social, intellectual and political interests in me. Then practicing law in Boston, helping to build a new law firm and to run it, kept me busy, as did our three children and active social life. I became deeply involved in local and national politics, and played an active role in the anti-Vietnam War movement (which even landed me on President Nixon's infamous Enemy's List). Most importantly, I continue to be involved in the struggle to try to control and eventually eliminate nuclear weapons. Though throughout this period I often considered resuming work on my Story, these other involvements always took precedence.

I am now way up in my eighties, fortunate still to be able to enjoy my life with Herta in the 63rd year of our marriage. The time has come, I have decided, to publish the Story of my first 27 years as it stands. That period deserves being captured for posterity, most other witnesses for it having departed by now. I trust that the major part of my life that followed will safely survive in the memories of our family and our friends.

Cambridge, MA

May 2007.

978-0-595-45365-8
0-595-45365-1